Lean on Civility

Thank you
for choosing
civility.

Dr. Lew Bayer

Lean on Civility

*Strategies for Changing Culture
in Manufacturing Workplaces*

Christian Masotti
Lewena Bayer

BUSINESS EXPERT PRESS
Leader in applied, concise business books

First published in 2021 by
Business Expert Press, LLC
222 East 46th Street, New York, NY 10017
www.businessexpertpress.com

ISBN-13: 978-1-95253-880-3 (paperback)
ISBN-13: 978-1-95253-881-0 (e-book)

Business Expert Press Human Resource Management and Organizational Behavior Collection

Collection ISSN: 1946-5637 (print)
Collection ISSN: 1946-5645 (electronic)

Cover image licensed by Ingram Image, StockPhotoSecrets.com
Cover and interior design by S4Carlisle Publishing Services Private Ltd., Chennai, India

First edition: 2021

10 9 8 7 6 5 4 3 2 1

Printed in the United States of America.

How to Use This Book

This book is intended as a toolkit and reference guide for workplace trainers, supervisors, consultants, and performance coaches who work with manufacturing teams. Newcomers to the industry might also benefit from reviewing the book as doing so would teach them what to expect and/or come to understand the industry they will be working in.

The content is best suited for delivery with entry-level or new-to-field employees who may not know much about manufacturing. However, supervisors and managers who support production teams should also review the book, and/or take the *Civility in Manufacturing Series* of courses online at www.civilityexperts.com. These include:

- Social Competence for Manufacturing Supervisors
- Manufacturing Civility
- Lean on Civility

Throughout the book you will see terms highlighted in bold. These terms can be found in the glossary in Chapter 10 and it is recommended that you learn them.

In addition, each chapter includes:

- Learning content with some questions for consideration
- Additional content for review
- Optional add-on assignments (listed in Chapter 9)
- Homework
- Recommended reading
- A short quiz to test your knowledge
- Advanced Thinking—preparatory excerpt at the end of each chapter for the next chapter

For the consideration questions, possible responses have been included in Chapter 9—Putting It All Together.

Description

In *Lean on Civility: Strategies for Changing Culture in Manufacturing Workplaces*, the authors explain how incorporating civility can drive success in your business. As a key component of workplace training, civility can have a significant impact on workplace culture and also increase measurable outputs related to continuous improvement—including but not limited to quality, efficiency, and cost. When organizations are deliberate and strategic about increasing supervisors' and managers' civility competencies in four key skill areas, they experience almost immediate improvements in interpersonal relationships, communication, morale, retention, trust, and productivity. *Lean on Civility: Strategies for Changing Culture in Manufacturing Workplaces* offers a practical tool kit—complete with strategies and tools (like the Masotti Feedback Method)—that you can take back to your workplace and implement immediately.

Keywords

manufacturing; workplace culture; civility; engagement; civility at work; workplace change

Contents

Lean on Civility

Chapter topic	Content covered	Learning objectives	Take-away and supports
1. The Culture of Manufacturing—Overview	Traditional manufacturing culture, command and control management style, benefits of traditional culture, consequences of traditional culture, history impacting manufacturing, predicted trends in manufacturing	Understand traditional manufacturing culture and how it was shaped. Identify need to change culture and factors that are influencing change. Learn general terms related to the manufacturing industry.	Words to know Recommended reading
2. The Business Case for Civility	Behaviors of disengaged employees, reasons for disengagement, change-readiness, need for knowledge workers, data logistics, definition of civility, benefits of civility, workplace civility metrics, civility assessment tools	Understand how civility impacts engagement and various key business metrics. Learn how fostering civility at work can impact metrics and workplace culture. Identify metrics that impact your current workplace. Consider how civility enables organizations to build trust and to manage data.	Terms to know Recommended reading Workplace Civility Metrics Survey© Civility Culture Compass Assessment©
3. Changing Workplace Culture	What is workplace culture, organizational behavior, the civility indicators iceberg, what is a change initiative, what is change-readiness, the Trident Approach	Understand what workplace culture is, how it is created, and how to change it. Apply the iceberg theory to understanding workplace culture relative to people treatment and civility.	Terms to know Recommended reading Perspectives on Change Lab 2019 Workplace Survey the workplace incivility filtering system

Figure 1 Book Summary Chart

(continued)

Chapter topic	Content covered	Learning objectives	Take-away and supports
4. Civility as a Continuous Improvement Strategy	What is continuous improvement, how is civility continuous improvement, the civility in practice model, indicators of civility, the civility culture continuum	Understand how and why civility is continuous improvement. Recognize the benefits of civility as continuous improvement. Learn what civility looks like in practice. Understand how civility can be measured on a continuum.	Terms to know Recommended reading Civility in practice model Indicators of civility chart The civility culture continuum
5. Embedding Civil Communication	Benefits of civil communication, what civil communication looks like, social acuity, how to be a civil communicator	Understand why civil communication is important. Learn about skills that underpin civility. Understand what social intelligence and social acuity are. Strategies for civil communication.	Terms to know Civility value chain Recommended reading Masotti Commonsense Social Competence Strategies Table (10)
6. AEIOU—the Masotti Method for Assessment and Observation	What is needs assessment, why do needs assessment, how to do needs assessment, AEIOU model, positive people treatment, relational wealth	Understanding what a needs assessment is. How to do a needs assessment. How to interpret value/relationships. Learn definition and examples of positive people treatment. Understand what relational wealth is.	Terms to know Civility culture compass assessment Recommended reading. Positive people treatment survey Bayer Relational value chart Masotti/Bayer need/value grid
7. The Masotti Methods	What is feedback, Masotti feedback method	Understanding the purpose of feedback. Learn benefits of giving feedback. What civil feedback looks like. Tips for eliminating bias and building trust.	Terms to know Recommended reading. Masotti method for feedback summary Relational value chart

Chapter topic	Content covered	Learning objectives	Take-away and supports
8. Making the Box Smaller— Reducing Variability Technique	Problem-solving using Masotti method	How to use the Masotti "make the box smaller" approach. Types of problem-solving strategies.	Terms to know Make the box smaller graphic Recommended reading
9. Putting It All Together	Answer keys, optional assignments	Review and compare learner responses with recommended responses. Test learner knowledge.	Add on: Stats and facts about Canadian manufacturing.
10. Tools You Can Use	Take-away and stand-alone supports.	Continue and share learning, e.g., in various environments, content can be adapted. Contact admin@civilityexperts.com for details about acquiring PDF forms.	Glossary Recommended Reading Sample Job Description Essential skills profile Sources and resources for each chapter Templates Various assessments Activity details

Figure 1 Continued

Templates and Forms

Please contact admin@civilityexperts.com for details about how you can get the forms and templates in PDF or other formats that you can customize for your workplace.

The Workplace Civility Metrics Survey® by Masotti and Bayer, 2019.

CHAPTER 1

The Culture of Manufacturing—Overview

Culture eats strategy for breakfast. Peter Drucker

"Just do your F@>djh;f?X job!"

"No one asked you to think."

"If you want to keep your job you better figure that S#%! out."

"That won't work here, just do as you're told."

"There's 30 guys smarter than you are waiting in line for this job. If you can't handle it, get the F&#I< out."

When I first started out in manufacturing in 1995, there is no question that it took some time to adjust to the strong language and often angry tone of the workplace communication. Marry that with the noise, oppressive and chronic deadlines, pressure to meet quotas, the harsh conditions, physical demands, and somewhat depressing overall demeanor of the employees, and it's sometimes hard to believe I've spent close to 24 years in the industry. It wasn't all bad, but overall, the above was my experience.

My first job was as an hourly employee on the **assembly line** of a production floor. I was a car seat assembler. I took the manufacturing job because it was nights and at that time, I was attending Broadcast Journalism courses during the day. After graduating from McGill University, playing professional football in the Canadian Football League, and travelling the world for 2 years, I was eager to start a career and work and was optimistic about learning manufacturing. My foray into the industry by way of the assembler role wasn't too hard, and after 5 years, I moved on to a contract position as production supervisor for Chrysler. I subsequently held positions as business unit leader and different roles in various other manufacturing organizations including Ford and Toyota. Most recently (since 2019 and at the time of writing this book), I am production coordinator at Arcelor Mittal, the largest steel manufacturing and mining company in the world. In addition, I work part-time as a conversions supervisor at Maple Leaf Sports & Entertainment (MLSE). MLSE manages Toronto Raptors (NBA), Toronto Maple Leafs (NHL), Live Nation Concerts, and the Toronto Football Club (MLS). Why this is important will become evident as you make your way through this book.

Early on, I came to understand that a caustic, and often psychologically toxic, management style was almost considered "normal" in manufacturing (At least this was the case in most of the organizations where I worked). Even though most of us, especially those who were new to the industry, realized that the conditions we were experiencing weren't typical of other workplaces, we didn't sit around and talk about which supervisor was being mean or who got yelled at. We didn't run off to Human Resources to complain when someone hurt our feelings. We just came to accept it. And if you didn't accept it, you didn't last long.

Over time we settled in. Incurring regular insults, being condescended to, yelled at, embarrassed, threatened, ignored, pushed to do more and to do it faster, was all part of the daily experience. And so, we carried on. We kept our mouths shut, put our heads down, and did the job. As such, I have observed and experienced, as many in the industry have, some of the obvious negative impacts of a power-oriented management style. It should be noted that the above captures my personal experience, and it was over the past 25 years.

Historically, this power-focused management style when applied to manufacturing is called "**command and control**."[1] In a command and control[2] style, a properly designated leader or commander exercises authority and directs subordinates. In directing others, the manager (and supervisors and other assigned leaders) essentially dictate everything: rules, tasks, timing, general workplace behavior, when you

---

[1] The Free Dictionary (Farlex). "Command and Control."13/02/2019 Published 2003-2020 www.thefreedictionary.com/command and control.
[2] Ibid.

can talk, eat, sit, take a break, make a change, ask a question, etc. Subordinates are not encouraged or allowed to make decisions on their own. Sometimes this is called the **C2 style**.[3]

As you would guess, there are often negative outcomes of command and control environments. For example:

- In many manufacturing organizations, employees who make it through the first few months tend to stay long-term. Transitioning new employees onto teams where some have been on the job for 20, 30, 40 years can be difficult. Typically, the longer-term employees like the "old way" and are resistant to change. As more and more employees representing the older generations—who traditionally stayed at one job their whole career—move on, the dynamic between the old guard who is left and the new kids on the block can be strained at best.
- In traditional command and control workplaces, there is little need for cross-training and talent development or encouraging high potential employees to develop their skills. Many long-term employees know one job really well and they just do that job. This works well as most manufacturing environments are also unions where traditionally there are very rigid expectations and lines in terms of who can do what.
- In organizations where there are many long-term employees, there is often a great amount of **"team" skills and knowledge** that are learned "on the job" by doing the job. If this tribal knowledge cannot be captured, succession planning is difficult and there are often wide skills gaps that need to be addressed. In this way, employees have a great deal of power, whether they perceive it or not. For example, in some cases, being a "gatekeeper" of sorts and withholding details about your job and how to do it can serve as job security. That is, the organization (or business unit anyway) may not be able to function without a specific employee or team remaining in that job.
- Traditionally manufacturing plants were set up in towns or smaller city centers, where the community was built around, and/or existed,

---

[3]Cambridge Dictionary. "Command and Control: Meaning in the Cambridge English Dictionary."13.02/2019 Published 2003-2020, https://dictionary.cambridge.org/dictionary/english/command-and-control.

because of the plant. As happens in small communities, word travels quickly and people learn about the culture of a workplace and organizations garner reputations. When the reputation includes harsh conditions, toxic work cultures, and incivility, it doesn't take long before the pool of potential new hires—typically young people in the community—actively look elsewhere for employment. As such, recruitment can be very difficult.

- Sometimes when individuals work under command and control for a long time, they can actually become conditioned not to think. And then, at times when they might need to react quickly, or think differently, or solve problems, they are less able to do so.

- When individuals have been on the job for a long time, especially if they've been in the same position, they can become very resistant to change. Sometimes this resistance is so strong, it becomes sabotaging.

What might surprise you if you've never worked in manufacturing is that, in spite of the negative aspects of command and control management style, not the least of which could be described as vastly uncivil **"people treatment,"** the job gets done. And this may be why trying to convince leadership that they need to do things differently has been, in most cases, a losing battle.

By way of fact, traditional command and control culture has endured in many manufacturing organizations because incivility aside, **key performance indicators** are usually met. In some cases, due to a predominant culture of fear and/or some inviting incentives, production goals even surpass expectations.

For those supervisors and managers who have survived in the industry long-term and have done so through this traditional power-focused leadership, there are perceived benefits to this style of management. For example, "command and control" environments often:

- require very little actual engagement on the part of employees—therefore less "inspiring" and "motivating" skills are required by leadership;

- enable a small number of "leaders" to control a large number of "followers"—this helps manage labor costs as well as limits the amount of leadership training and development an organization needs to invest in;

- require very little attention to people issues, for example, emotions, reactions to change;
- outline clear reporting paths—hierarchy—so everyone knows his or her place and related accountabilities;
- maintain control, to a large degree, of processes and costs, as well as safety—for example, when there is little deviation allowable from the processes and plan, there is very little deviation in behavior, costs, and risk;
- eliminate the need for a lot of cross-team or up/down communication or discussion—orders are given and passed along the appropriate channels;
- facilitate successful change, specifically related to processes and regulated activities;
- create silos, which many assume to always be a bad thing, but which in fact can:
  - support clear boundaries so accountabilities, specifically, permissions and roles, need not be repeatedly taught or discussed;
  - foster team pride, that is, high morale and engagement within the silo;
  - create filters that enable sifting out only the data important to the immediate team; for example, there is clarity about what is pertinent and what is not and there are frequently fewer delays in production;
  - create levels of trust sufficient such that the silo team shares information and "on the job" (tribal and often closely guarded) information that can be used appropriately because competence is assumed within the silo team.

So, you may be wondering—if the plant teams are producing, targets are being reached, and even safety goals are being achieved, why mess with a good thing? Maybe it is a tough environment, and occasionally leadership is hard on the employees, so what? No workplace has perfect culture so why not just leave things alone?

The fact is, on the surface, things do seem to work. But at what cost? When you take a closer look and examine metrics (and review the research) like workplace wellness, **retention**,[4] long-term disability (e.g., stress related), specific aspects of efficiency, safety, and **engagement**, it becomes evident pretty quickly that there are significant negative long-term impacts to command and control environments—particularly where the overall communication style can be described as overtly, and unnecessarily, uncivil. We will take a closer look at some of these less measured impacts of incivility in Chapter 2, "The Business Case for Civility."

Let's first take a look at influences that have impacted manufacturing workplace culture in the past as well as consider how some forecasted trends will impact manufacturing in the future.

Pivotal Changes That Impacted Manufacturing in the Past

The industrial revolution—the era in which machines changed the way people made things—wouldn't be possible without technological advancement. In the case of manufacturing, it was the creation of the steam engine. Prior to this, manufacturing was a household activity, accomplished using hand tools or rudimentary machines. While early mills were operated using wind or waterpower, the development of the steam engine made it possible to develop a factory virtually anywhere. This kicked off an era of collaboration and a move to special-purpose machinery and mass production in factories, mills, and mines. This initiated a bold new technological phase of productivity and efficiency.

With the steam engine came the ability to produce things in large quantities. Mass production methods—establishing a production system by using physical labor to design, produce, and assemble standardized parts—quickly become a way of life. But it was American innovator Henry Ford who revolutionized mass production with his development of the assembly line for the Model T automobile in the early 1900s. In this system, every worker was given a specific task and built upon each other's work to create a vehicle, section by section. It kick-started the industrial complex and was the advent of modern mass production.

---

[4]Weber and Shadwick. https://www.webershandwick.com/wp-content/uploads/2018/04/Civility-in-Business-Exec-Summary-1.pdf 12/12/2018 Published 2013

The mid-1950s saw the rise of **automation** and the information age. Advances in computer science translated into the creation of large-scale, high-speed computing machines. The first of its kind was the Univac 1101 or ERA 1101—a massive machine that used vacuum tubes, console type-writers, and magnetic tape to compute.

By the end of the 1950s, the creation of the transistor transformed the industry. Manufacturers could now replace costly, inefficient vacuum tubes in computing equipment. This meant the early bulky computer ma-chines could be developed into smaller, compact devices that were more efficient. Most importantly, the information age ushered in an innova-tive workforce, one that used automation and computerization to help boost productivity, develop products faster, and heighten consumer con-sumption by changing the way we accessed, presented, and manipulated information.[5]

For Consideration: Forecasted Trends Influences[6]

In reviewing the three significant events that changed manufacturing, how would you describe how these events impacted **workplace culture** in manufacturing organizations?

Topic 1: Industry 4.0 Comes of Age

The growth of "Industry 4.0" has been a widely discussed topic since 2017 and its steep upward trajectory is certainly going to continue. For example, the International Federation of Robotics (IFR) predicts that more than 1.7 million new industrial robots will be installed in factories worldwide by 2020, representing an annual growth rate of 14 percent.

---

[5]R. Sabio. 2017. "4 Pivotal Moments in History That Changed the Way We Make Things," *HuffPost Canada*. www.huffingtonpost.ca/2017/02/09/manufacturing-history_n_14664146.html (Updated February 22, 2017).

[6]D. York. January 10, 2018. "Manufacturing Sector Set for Significant Change in 2018," *Logistics\Manufacturing Global*. www.manufacturingglobal.com/logistics/manufacturing-sector-set-significant-change-2018.

Essentially, Industry 4.0 is about combining artificial intelligence and data science to realize the potential of the **Internet of Things (IoT)**, but just having access to large pools of information is no longer enough. The important thing that manufacturers need to take advantage of over the coming years is using that data to gain insight, inform decisions, and drive better business outcomes.

As more and more "smart" devices have been integrated into organizations since 2018, Industry 4.0 will continue to dominate the manufacturing industry, offering valuable benefits including predictive maintenance of machinery and increased levels of automation to help manufacturers optimize their operations. One example of this is for inventory control of spares and raw materials. Sensors are being used to identify stock levels and, based on historical information, automate the replenishment of these items. This innovation decreases production downtime and ensures an optimized delivery schedule.

Keeping up with this trend is about being able to build upon a loop of intelligence that feeds into a cycle of continuous improvement. In layman's terms, this involves gathering as much data as possible, turning this data into insight, and finally into intelligence which can be used to improve business processes.

This is the mindset manufacturers should adopt when it comes to **Enterprise Resource Planning (ERP).** However, making the move towards a smarter ERP system can require a cultural shift for manufacturers as well as for financial investment.

ERP systems are already collecting more business data than ever before but making sense of this data and taking action on it will be the key differentiator in the year ahead.

Question: How do you think this trend will impact workplace culture in manufacturing organizations?

Topic 2: Customer Experience Is King

With the increasing amount of data being created by Industry 4.0 comes the opportunity to significantly enhance the customer experience.

This is an area that, thanks to increasingly competitive business landscapes, is now more important than ever. Success beyond 2020 will boil down to how well companies can differentiate themselves from the rest and focusing on the customer journey will be a key aspect.

Customers today expect the same service in their work life as they get in their personal life, which means "business-to-business" companies need to start behaving more like "business-to-consumer" ones and treat the customer experience as sacred. For example, people are used to features such as same-day delivery and one-click ordering in their personal lives, which is making them more demanding in their professional capacities.

For manufacturers dealing with a complex supply chain, a robust and modern ERP system is now widely recognized as playing a crucial role in improving the customer experience. IDC research reports that 85 percent of manufacturers with more than 5,000 employees identify ERP as being a vital platform to delivering positive customer experiences.[7]

A flexible, fully integrated ERP system that streamlines operational processes and connects back-office with front-office functions throughout the lifetime of an asset or product enables manufacturers to offer a much higher level of service—a level of service that they are able to charge more for and will set them well apart from their competitors.

Question: What types of new processes do you think will have to be implemented to help manage the people side of these new high-tech systems?

Topic 3: AI-Driven Future

Linked to improving the customer experience is the role of artificial intelligence (AI), which is set to have a profound impact on ERP systems moving towards 2025 and beyond in several diverse ways.

For example, AI-driven ERP is being used to create dynamic workflows that learn the various ways in which an organization and its employees interact with the software, before suggesting different optimizations for individual users.

In terms of improving customer service and support, AI is, for example, allowing businesses to provide always-on customer service that

---

[7]IDC. n.d. "Insights—Home." www.idc.com/prodserv/insights/#manufacturing.

isn't constrained by time zones or holidays. It is also quickly scalable and enables an unparalleled level of personalization throughout the customer journey.

Furthermore, AI in the form of predictive analytics can be used to produce deeper insights for specific business outcomes and make more sense of the mountains of data manufacturers are now collecting and storing.

More use cases will become apparent as the technology continues to develop, but what's already clear is that the potential of AI when it comes to ERP is significant.

With political and economic upheavals on the horizon, businesses are facing an unclear future. There are turbulent times ahead, but those organizations that concentrate on making themselves smart and agile will be the ones that are best positioned to take advantage of growth opportunities well beyond 2020.

For manufacturers, this process starts by ensuring that internal software systems are fully supported with the latest updates, thereby enabling them to react to change and view the likes of Brexit and GDPR as opportunities rather than threats.

Question: Given that many manufacturing organizations have large numbers of long-term employees who are sometimes resistant to change, what plan would you put in place to try to offset the potential fear, lack of change readiness, and general resistance to AI in the workplace?

In addition to the three trends identified by Manufacturing Global, field research by the Civility Experts Inc. international team suggests that the following are the top issues or challenges facing manufacturing organizations as we head towards 2025 and into the next decade:

- Lack of skilled labor, for example, there is a growing manufacturing skills gap
- Challenges due to a multi-generational workforce; specifically, attracting and retaining employees and meeting expectations for employee satisfaction
- Lack of "culture for quality," for example, quality standards issues; specifically, a need to eliminate closed-loop quality management, for example, problems being solved within silos but not shared or applied to the larger organization

- Balancing project deadlines while still producing quality products; specifically, providing advanced project management and managing lower costs and rising quality, especially related to international or overseas suppliers
- Need for better supply-chain visibility and production workflow to improve performance and reduce costs (competitive pricing/increase revenue growth)
- Ability to effectively measure quality metrics and performance indicators; specifically, maximizing technological intelligence and data mining and ensuring readiness to handle exponential data growth
- Poor customer service, for example, related to self-service trends (use of technology), which result in a need to be customer-adaptive
- Difficulties integrating old with new technologies while maintaining or improving quality and efficiencies, for example, cybersecurity
- Time loss due to regional and national compliance requirements
- Maintaining and monitoring safety mindset amidst increasing automation

See Chapter 9 for Optional Assignment.

Words to Know

- Assembly line
- Command and control
- Tribal skills and knowledge
- People treatment
- Key performance indicators
- Retention
- Engagement
- Industrial revolution
- Automation
- Transistor
- Workplace culture
- Internet of Things
- Enterprise Resource Planning (ERP)

For Review

1. What are the possible benefits of a command and control management style?
2. Why do you think the command and control management style was/is prevalent in many manufacturing organizations?
3. What trends and influences might prompt organizations to move away from a power-focused management style?

How Much Do You Remember?

1. Traditional power-focused management style in manufacturing has resulted in what kind of workplace culture?
   a. Overt controlling
   b. Commander as leader
   c. Command and control
   d. None of the above
2. Team knowledge is:
   a. information specific to the first manufacturing companies ever created
   b. knowledge about processes that only the employees know
   c. knowledge learning on the job that isn't known to everyone
   d. a and b
3. Traditional power-focused manufacturing workplace culture can create levels of trust sufficient such that the silo team shares information and "on the job" information that can be used appropriately because competence is assumed within the silo team. True or False?
4. Provide two examples of pivotal changes or events in history that impacted manufacturing.

Recommended Reading

Norman, D. 2013. *The Design of Everyday Things: Revised and Expanded Edition Paperback*. Philadelphia, PA: Basic Book, Perseus Books Group.

Homework Assignment

Review the article below and write a 500 to 750-word briefing note on the article including your viewpoint on how these trends will impact manufacturing and what you would do to offset the potential impacts.

Current Trends and Changes Expected to Impact Manufacturing

The current and future manufacturing age is upon us with the rise of the *cyber-physical system* (CPS). Also referred to as the era of *Internet of Things (IoT)*, the "*connected factory*" or Industry 4.0, it's a technology that allows machines to talk to each other over a secure IT network. That data conversation makes manufacturers more efficient by presenting information, in real time, which allows them to make data-based decisions.

Manufacturers are increasingly leveraging the Internet of Things (IoT), which entails the interconnection of unique devices within an existing Internet infrastructure, to achieve a variety of goals including cost reduction, increased efficiency, improved safety, meeting compliance requirements, and product innovation. IoT's existence is primarily due to three factors: widely available Internet access, smaller sensors, and cloud computing.

Roughly 63 percent of manufacturers believe that applying IoT to products will increase profitability over the next 5 years and are set to invest $267 billion in IoT by 2020.[8]

A breakdown in critical equipment is costly to manufacturers both in terms of repairs as well as downtime and loss of productivity. According to Information Technology Intelligence Consulting, 98 percent of organizations say a single hour of downtime costs over $100,000. Ensuring that all equipment is functioning optimally therefore remains a key priority for manufacturers, many of whom are turning to predictive maintenance technology to do so.

Widespread adoption of predictive maintenance technologies could reduce companies' maintenance costs by 20 percent, reduce unplanned

---

[8]Hitachi Solutions. February 7, 2019. "10 Trends That Will Dominate Manufacturing Trends in 2019." https://us.hitachi-solutions.com/blog/top-manufacturing-trends/.

outages by 50 percent, and extend machinery life by years, according to management consulting firm McKinsey & Company.[9]

Remaining competitive means delivering more value to your customers than your competitors. While pricing is extremely important, savvy manufacturers will continue to distance themselves from price wars by leveraging new technology that simplifies supply chain management, which in turn delivers many competitive benefits. These benefits include being able to operate your business more efficiently, more visibility and control over inventory, reduction of operational costs, and improved customer satisfaction and retention.

Today's supply chain technology solutions address manufacturing needs in a variety of areas, including:

- Manufacturing optimization
- Logistics optimization
- Sales and operations planning
- Product lifecycle management
- Business intelligence
- Network and inventory optimization
- RFID
- Procurement

A third of over 2,000 industrial companies have digitized their supply chains while nearly three-quarters expect to by 2020, according to PwC.[10] Many manufacturers who traditionally had a B2B business model are shifting to a B2B2C (business-to-business-to-consumer) model due to the many benefits selling directly to consumers provides including:

- **Increased profit:** You get the full manufacturer's suggested retail price (MSRP) rather than wholesale prices for your products.

---

[9]J. Manyika. June 2017. "A Future That Works: AI, Automation, Employment, and Productivity," Extracts from McKinsey Global Institute Research. www.jbs.cam.ac.uk/fileadmin/user_upload/research/centres/risk/downloads/170622-slides-manyika.pdf.
[10]PricewaterhouseCoopers. n.d. "Strategy& PwC." www.strategyand.pwc.com/.

- **Faster time to market:** You can prototype, test, and get products to market quickly instead of contending with the lengthy traditional retail sales cycle that requires locked-down product development far ahead of order and delivery. This agility gives you a competitive edge.
- **Brand control:** You own your brand. It won't be diluted or misrepresented by third parties.
- **Price control:** You can reinforce your MSRP.
- **Better customer data:** Selling direct to customers allows you to collect data about them that ultimately results in better products, stronger relationships, and increased sales.

To effectively sell direct to consumers you'll need to select a platform for your e-commerce operations that supports both your B2B and B2C sales platforms. It will have to deliver on order fulfillment and tracking, secure payments, customer service management, and sales and marketing activity tracking while providing a 360° view of all your B2B and B2C customer interactions.[11]

Advanced Thinking—Preparing for Chapter 2

My assessment as someone currently working in the field, is that one of the key challenges manufacturing organizations face is related to information. Specifically, how do supervisor or managers get ALL the information they need, WHEN they need it, in the format and in the WAY they need it? Let's call this "data logistics."

And how do they do this so that the information is still relevant by the time they figure out what to do with it? Let's call this "real-time data." Keeping up with modern technology requires almost constant access to immediate data.

In addition to being immediate, timely, accessible, mobile, and presentable in various ways, for example, visual, in print, as image, or video, as statistical output, etc., to whomever might need it, anywhere in the

---

[11]Hitachi Solutions. February 7, 2019. "10 Trends That Will Dominate Manufacturing Trends in 2019." https://us.hitachi-solutions.com/blog/top-manufacturing-trends/.

plant, the data also has to be translatable—that is, simple and at the same time complex enough to be used by different people for different purposes.

The above represents a problem which, left unsolved, can result in critical, costly impacts to an organization.

The reality is, if a supervisor is trying to achieve collection of this data alone, he or she will very rarely be able to gather all the data needed in real time. The solution is…leaders at any level need collaboration and everyone on the team must be a systems thinker. All employees at all levels must understand that they have information that is necessary and useful to other employees in the business. And they must be willing to share that information. However, you can be sure that leaders or supervisors will not be getting the cooperation they need from the production team if they are consistently uncivil with their team members. People—especially leaders—must have built ongoing civil, trusting relationships with all members of the team. By doing this, when the time comes for sharing and collaborating, the data and information is shared more readily because there is mutual respect and alignment between the individual roles and organizational goals. When there is effective collaboration, people see that success, knowledge, and data (good or bad) in one area of the business fosters and supports success, knowledge, and data, in other aspects of the business.

What do you think about this?

CHAPTER 2

The Business Case
for Civility

*In uncivil workplaces, it is possible to meet your production goals, despite a **toxic culture**, but there is ALWAYS collateral damage. And over time, the costs of this collateral damage can be prohibitive. Civility helps lower these costs.*

—Christian Masotti

- Calling in sick
- Leaving early
- Taking extra or longer breaks
- Skipping meetings
- Badmouthing others
- Breaching confidentiality, e.g., sharing information or e-mails, that should not be shared
- Failing to respond to communications
- Withholding information
- Ignoring or avoiding others
- Refusing to listen to the viewpoints of others
- Being present but "off," e.g., being distracted
- Failing to exhibit common courtesies, e.g., saying hello, thank you, please
- Forwarding others' e-mail to make them look bad
- Failing to return phone calls or respond to e-mails
- Withholding information
- Refusing to participate or cooperate
- Working slower
- Avoiding asking questions or engaging others

These are just a few of the damaging behaviors that one out of every five employees in the workplace is engaging in, or experiencing, EVERY week. And according to research conducted by American workplace culture researcher Christine Porath, these behaviors, due to the stress they cause, cost U.S. companies an estimated 350 billion annually.[1] Clearly, these indicators of incivility at work are not contained to U.S. companies. Research shows that companies around the world are experiencing similar issues. Alarmingly, studies also show that the percentage of employees who report being treated rudely by colleagues at least once a month has risen by 13 percent over the past 20 years.[2]

Furthermore, research verifies that incivility at work impacts innovation, team orientation, service standards, retention, safety, efficiency, workplace health, workplace learning, engagement, and profitability. These issues are prevalent across sectors.

Incivility at work is real in workplaces all over the globe. And it's real in manufacturing.

In case you did not know, a Gallup *State of the American Workplace* report, found that 75 percent of manufacturing workers are disengaged at work. In fact, the manufacturing industry, according to the Gallup report, is the least engaged occupation across all sectors.

If, as is the case in other sectors, the dissatisfaction reported by 80 percent of disengaged employees is a result of the factors listed below, manufacturing employers should be concerned.

- Perception of being undervalued
- Anger at being underpaid, e.g., based on competitors and/or industry averages
- Feeling of being overtly disrespected
- Fear about losing one's job
- Inability to meet expectations due to lack of training or tools
- Knowledge that the company does not care about the employees, e.g., as indicated by lack of safety

---

[1]C. Porath, and C. Pearson. January–February 2013. "The Price of Incivility," *Harvard Business Review*. https://hbr.org/2013/01/the-price-of-incivility.06/03/2019
[2]Ibid.

- Lack of transparency and honesty in communications
- Unfairness and/or inequity in policy and practice
- Experience of generally being treated badly

Notably, 80 percent of people are dissatisfied with their jobs.[3]

Twenty five percent of employees say work is their main source of stress and 40 percent say their job is "very or extremely stressful."[4] This stress impacts our health—for example, in the UK, over 13 million working days are lost every year because of stress. Stress is believed to trigger 70 percent of visits to doctors, and 85 percent of serious illnesses.[5]

Work is killing us. In Japan, shockingly, 10,000 workers per year literally drop dead at their desks as a result of 60- to 70-hour work weeks in Japan. This phenomenon is known as "**karoshi.**"[6]

Work demands are impacting our work–life balance; for example, each year the average American spends over 100 hours commuting[7] and 64 percent of Americans canceled vacations last year. One-third did it for work-related reasons even though most felt they were more in need of a vacation than the year before.[8] It's hard to catch up on your life if you are losing time just getting to work, and hard to de-stress if you can't take a vacation.

Stress at work impacts our relationships. According to the Human Solutions Report, *Under Pressure*, respondents indicated that on average job stress accounted for 73 percent of their overall life stress. Further,

[3]R. Premack. August 2, 2018. "17 Seriously Disturbing Facts about Your Job," *Business Insider*. www.businessinsider.com/disturbing-facts-about-your-job-2011-2?op=1 #ixzz3XCZH6nbq.04/08/2018

[4]L. Worrall, and C.L. Cooper. 2006. *The Quality of Working Life: Managers Health and Well-Being: Executive Summary* (London: Chartered Management Institute).

[5]Health and Safety Executive. 2019. "Working Days Lost in Great Britain." www.hse .gov.uk/statistics/dayslost.htm (accessed October 30, 2019). 14/12/2019

[6]The Economist. December 19, 2007. "Jobs for Life." www.economist.com/ asia/2007/12/19/jobs-for-life. 04/08/2019

[7]R. Longley. 2017. "Americans Spend over 100 Hours a Year Commuting," *ThoughtCo*. http://usgovinfo.about.com/od/censusandstatistics/a/commutetimes.htm (Updated July 29, 2017). 05/08/2019

[8]A. Shontell. September 13, 2010. "64% of Americans Canceled Their Vacations This Year," *Business Insider*. www.businessinsider.com/64-canceled-vacation-this -year-2010-9.04/08/2019

59 percent of respondents said that the quality of their home and family life was sometimes impacted by job stress and 16 percent said that job stress frequently impacted their personal and family life.[9]

With a whopping 96 percent of employees polled in a workplace study conducted by Pearson and Porath[10] experiencing rudeness at work, and knowing that the majority of people say stress at work is the largest contributor to their overall stress, it's not unreasonable to infer that rudeness is contributing to the stress. And, it's easy to see that work simply is not much fun for a lot of people.

If you are wondering how or why all of this impacts manufacturing specifically, consider for example, some of the more obvious negative outcomes of the traditional manufacturing command and control management approach—employees feeling diminished, stressed, and in cases powerless. Aside from these outcomes of day-to-day incivility, consider the extent to which the ongoing mental, physical, and even emotional stress all common in traditional manufacturing workplace cultures, potentially impacts the following behaviors that are required on the job in manufacturing:

- Paying attention, e.g., to safety issues
- Trusting others, e.g., to keep you safe
- Sharing information, e.g., team knowledge
- Observing intelligently, e.g., to identify problems
- Thinking critically, e.g., to solve problems

As you might guess, it is going to be more difficult to achieve key performance metrics—including safety, which is critical—if employees do not pay attention, trust, share, observe, or think on the job.

The bottom line is that employees' overall experience at work, which is largely influenced by how managers, supervisors, and leaders treat them,

---

[9]Graham Lowe. April 4, 2007. "Under Pressure: Implications of Work-Life Balance and Job Stress." https://grahamlowe.ca/reports/under-pressure-implications-of-work-life-balance-and-job-stress/. 03/06/2019

[10]C. Porath, and C. Pearson. January–February 2013. "The Price of Incivility," *Harvard Business Review*. https://hbr.org/2013/01/the-price-of-incivility. 06/08/2019

matters. It matters a lot. In fact, according to Michelle McQuaid, a leading expert in positive psychology, 65 percent of working adults said a better boss would make them happy. Only 35 percent said a raise would do the same.

And it's not just the people treatment component of manufacturing workplace culture that needs to change. Clearly the industry is managing chronic and significant change in other ways as well. For example, as we move towards 2030, manufacturing organizations will need to manage the trends and influences discussed in Chapter 1 including, but not limited to:

- Increased automation
- Increased demand for data and shifts in how that data is used
- Unpredictable shifts in legislation and regulation related to sourcing and international trade
- Ever-changing shifts in availability, longevity, and expectations of a diminishing labor pool
- Ongoing demand to leverage and build both leadership and front-line skills

What does all this mean? Well, to begin with, manufacturing organizations need to be "change-ready." This includes:

A) Assessing the factors, issues, changes, and influences that impact their business as well as the competencies needed to address those issues, changes, and influences
B) Planning how to address the items outlined for a) above
C) Training to the skills gaps identified related to the competencies identified in a) above; to mitigate the ongoing and increasing costs of training, they need to:
  - leverage the talents and potential of existing teams, e.g., by building trust such that people share information and support each other;
  - learn continuously, e.g., embedding a culture of learning into their workplaces where individuals take responsibility for their own learning;
  - decrease stress at work towards increasing retention and productivity, e.g., by embedding civility into their practices and policies.

D) Measuring the impact of training, the transfer of the skill gain to the organization, and the impact of the transfer to the bottom-line metrics

For Consideration: Data Logistics and Real-Time Data

IMPORTANT: In a recent Forbes survey of 130 manufacturers, the most important skill for the next generation of employees is data analysis.

Additionally, as the sector braces for a shortfall of skilled labor, most manufacturers understand that they not only need to find ways to keep their current employees, they also need to find a way to entice a new breed of "knowledge workers."

"**Knowledge workers**" are self-directed individuals who frequently have education, experience, and options, as well as access to myriad sources of information about their rights, reasonable accommodation, and respectful workplace policy. Trying to manage this cohort with an outdated, hierarchical, process-focused approach will come at a high cost. To offset attrition, poor morale, safety and productivity issues, and to keep up with technologies such as artificial intelligence (AI), robotics, and Internet of Things (IoT), progressive manufacturing organizations are looking at civility as a viable solution for changing workplace culture.

While it was predicted that technology would decrease employment opportunities in manufacturing, job openings have been growing at double-digit rates since mid-2017 and are nearing the historical peak recorded in 2001. According to research conducted by Deloitte and The Manufacturing Institute there is a widening gap between the jobs that need to be filled and the skilled talent pool capable of filling them. The Deloitte study reveals that the skills gap may leave an estimated 2.4 million positions unfilled between 2018 and 2028, with a potential economic impact of 2.5 trillion. Further, the study shows that the positions relating to digital talent, skilled production, and operational managers may be three times as difficult to fill in the next 3 years.[11] With recruitment a potential

---

[11]S. Pajula, US Industries, and Deloitte LLP. 2020. "2018 Skills Gap in Manufacturing Study," *Deloitte United States*.06/04/2019www2.deloitte.com/us/en/pages/manufacturing/articles/future-of-manufacturing-skills-gap-study.html (accessed April 24, 2020).

and significant challenge, manufacturers would be wise to work harder to retain their current employees. And if the cause of low retention is toxicity in the workplace, shifting to a more civil workplace culture offers a possible solution.

In the Advanced Thinking segment at the end of Chapter 1, I suggested that, based on my current experience in the field, one of the key challenges manufacturing organizations face is related to information. Specifically, how do supervisor and managers get ALL the information they need, WHEN they need it, in the format and in the WAY they need it? Let's call this "data logistics."

And I also asked, "How do supervisors or managers do this so that the information is still relevant by the time they figure out what to do with it?" Let's call this "real-time data." My recommended solution to what I perceive as a critical problem is that people generally, but especially leaders, must have built ongoing civil, trusting relationships with all members of the team. By doing this, when the time comes for sharing and collaborating, the data and information is shared more readily because there is mutual respect and alignment between the individual roles and organizational goals.

Questions

A) **What specific aspects of leadership (supervisor/manager) behavior do you think can impact an employee's experience such that an employee will trust that leader?**

B) **How and why do you think high levels of trust might support the needs of "knowledge workers"?**

C) **How would building trust and having a team of "knowledge workers" be important relative to data logistics and real-time data?**

At this point, you should have a sense of the costs and consequences of incivility and as such, have a general understanding of the business case for civility. The next step is having a clear understanding of what civility is.

Many people have adopted a dictionary definition of civility and so understand the word to mean "politeness" or "manners" or "reasonable behavior" This understanding might be okay in terms of day-to-day interactions but when discussing civility in the workplace, these over-simplified definitions of civility allow for far too much subjectivity to be useful. Furthermore, if you identify civility in this way, it is likely going to be difficult to see how civility can have an immediate and significant impact on your bottom line, specifically in a manufacturing environment.

Words matter. And so, to ensure people recognize civility training as a real solution, it's helpful to define the term in a way that illustrates how civility is a measurable competency. For our purposes in this book, we have adopted the Civility Experts Inc. definition of civility. Civility Experts Inc., founded in 1999 by Lew Bayer, is internationally recognized as a leader in the field and their definition has been endorsed as part of the National Occupational Standards for Civility Practitioner framework, adopted by International Civility Trainers' Consortium for certification purposes, and used by thousands of civility trainers around the globe.

Civility Experts Inc. defines civility as:

- a conscious awareness of the impact of one's thoughts, actions, words, and intentions on others; combined with,
- a continuous acknowledgement of one's responsibility to ease the experience of others (e.g., through restraint, kindness, non-judgment, respect, and courtesy); and,
- a consistent effort to adopt and exhibit civil behavior as a non-negotiable point of one's character.

By this definition, **conscious awareness** makes the point that it's not enough to extend courtesy out of habit, and it's not a good enough excuse when you do not extend appropriate consideration to say you weren't aware or weren't paying attention. When we are conscious of the impact of our thoughts and words and actions, when we focus and attend to our surroundings, we are reminded that we have the power to impact people and situations and communications. In attending, we become thoughtful and when we are thoughtful, we become thinkers. As Dr. Forni says in his latest book, *The Thinking Life—How to Thrive in the Age of Distraction*, "You are thoughtful if you are a thinker, but you are also thoughtful if you are considerate." (In workplaces, this aspect of thinking ties to a recognition of accountability as well as to problem-solving.)

Continuous acknowledgement of one's responsibility references ethics and the inherent human dignity of others. Consideration of human dignity is in fact embedded in Human Rights and Labor legislations. In the workplace, this responsibility ties to personal responsibility and includes obligations related to common courtesy, non-judgment, and restraint, regardless of whether they are written into a job description or code of conduct.

Consistent effort relates to understanding that when workplace standards are at issue, as happens in most workplaces, being civil some of the time isn't enough. Civility must be an everyday, all-day endeavor. This is essential to building trust.

> Choosing civility has to become our default thinking pattern. It must become embedded in the workplace culture such that it becomes a key part of the character of the organization and a reflection of the character of the people who make up the organization, consistency in choosing civility is critical to changing workplace culture.[12]

With an understanding, then, of what civility is and accepting the fact that the majority of manufacturing workplaces manage to survive despite various degrees of dysfunctionality and incivility, imagine how much more productive and profitable these organizations could be if they incorporated civility into their policies and practices.

A growing body of research shows that there are measurable, often long-term benefits to civility in the workplace. These benefits include, but are not limited to:

- Increased retention
- Improved safety
- Greater individual and organizational adaptive capacity
- Employee autonomy
- Individual skills mastery and increased confidence

---

[12]Lew Bayer. CEO Civility Experts Inc. 2016

- More effective goal-setting
- Better alignment of daily activity with organizational goals
- More accountability
- Greater consistency in service delivery
- Increased respect in the workplace
- More frequent exhibition of common courtesies
- Generalized reciprocity
- More civil discourse
- Increased acceptance of diversity
- Greater team-orientation
- More collaboration
- Increased innovation
- Improved thinking skills
- Improved self-respect
- More self-directed learning
- Improved culture of learning
- Greater change-readiness
- Improved engagement
- Higher understanding of shared purpose
- Increased trust
- More responsibility-taking
- Higher self-rated "happy at work" scores
- Employee hardiness
- Increased psychological safety
- Better stress management
- Increased exercising of restraint
- Improved morale
- More efficient communication

Depending on the application, organizational civility initiatives can be complex endeavors. (We discuss this in more detail in Chapter 3). However, incorporating aspects of civility into communication codes, feedback approaches, and day-to-day interaction is not terribly costly or time-consuming, and even the small changes and strategies suggested in the next few chapters can go a long way towards building a culture of civility in manufacturing workplaces.

See Chapter 9 for Optional Assignment.

Words to Know

- Incivility
- Toxic culture
- People treatment
- Continuous improvement
- Karoshi
- Knowledge worker
- Civility

How Much Do You Remember?

1. Stress at work accounts for what percentage of overall life stress (according to Quality of Life report)?
   a. 10 percent
   b. 40 percent
   c. 73 percent
   d. 67 percent

2. Gallup *State of the American Workplace* report found that what percentage of employees in manufacturing environments are disengaged?
   a. 75 percent
   b. 25 percent
   c. 39 percent
   d. 72 percent

3. The term for literally dropping dead at work is called:
   a. katsume
   b. karoshi
   c. burnout
   d. disintegration

4. A knowledge worker is:
   a. an employee who may know how to do aspects of many jobs
   b. employees who are continuous learners
   c. employees who take responsibility for their own learning
   d. all the above

For Review

That employees trust their leaders is crucial to building a culture of civility in a workplace. Many people do not realize that civility is a measurable competency and that you can, in fact, train people to be civil. But the work team must want to change and build a better culture before civility training can have an impact.

In many organizations, the work groups at all levels have become so accustomed to a work style and workplace culture that they may not even be conscious of how uncivil the workplace is. Based on 20 years of field research, Masotti and Bayer have devised the *Workplace Civility Metrics Survey*® which identifies 32 measurable elements that indicate overall levels of civility. The elements are not listed in order of priority or relevance, but leaders are encouraged to highlight the elements that align with their organizational goals.

A higher score indicates a more positive or civil workplace culture and a lower score indicates incivility. Based on the Civility Experts Inc. research, lower scores are often indicative of equally low levels of trust.

Element	Average score 0 (low) and 10 (high)
1. Retention—general /overall	
2. Organizational capacity, e.g., maximizing resources	
3. Employee autonomy, e.g., at production level	
4. Individual skills mastery and confidence	
5. Effective goal setting, e.g., at production level	
6. Alignment of daily activity with organizational goals	
7. Accountability—generally	
8. Consistency in service delivery	
9. Respect in the workplace, e.g., if respect = value, to what extent is each individual valued equally?	
10. Exhibition of common courtesies	
11. Generalized reciprocity—that is, doing for others with no expectation of return, and doing things that are not required by the job description	
12. Civil discourse, e.g., monitored tone, appropriate turn-taking, moderate volume, avoidance of harsh words or profanity	
13. Acceptance of diversity	
14. Team-orientation without being constantly directed to be a team	

Element	Average score 0 (low) and 10 (high)
15. Volunteer collaboration	
16. Innovation	
17. Thinking skills, e.g., effective decision-making, measured risk-taking	
18. Self-respect, e.g., standing up for what one believes is right (courage on the job)	
19. Self-directed learning, e.g., making independent choices to seek learning	
20. Culture of learning—encouraged by leaders and peers to pursue learning	
21. Change readiness—open to change and able to adapt in a timely and effective way	
22. Engagement—defined as personal "buy-in" and trust of organization	
23. Understanding of shared purpose	
24. Overall trust	
25. Responsibility-taking without having to be directed, e.g., claiming errors or apologizing	
26. Self-rated "happy at work" scores	
27. Hardiness, e.g., physical bounce-back ability to withstand high physical stress	
28. Psychological safety, e.g., extent to which employee would feel okay stating personal issues related to heath or otherwise	
29. Stress management, e.g., did the company offer supports?	
30. Restraint, e.g., did people stop and think before acting?	
31. Overall morale	
32. Efficient (timely and concise) communication	

Figure 2 Workplace Civility Metrics Survey©, Masotti & Bayer 2019

As an alternative to the Civility Metrics Survey, and if you need to conduct a broader, general situational analysis, you can visit www.Civilityexperts.com and complete the Civility Culture Compass Assessment© to understand how your organization ranks in four core civility competency areas: social intelligence, cultural competence, systems thinking, and continuous learning; and on four conditions that predict success of civility initiatives: change, readiness, engagement, and alignment.

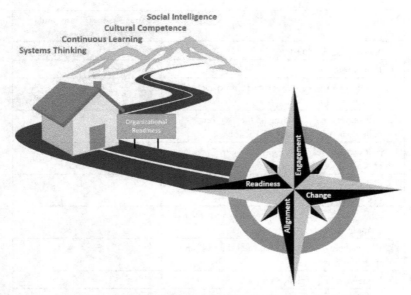

Figure 3 Civility Culture Compass©, Civility Experts Inc. 2016

Recommended Reading

Gallup 2020. "State of the American Workplace." www.gallup
.com/workplace/285818/state-american-workplace-report.aspx
(February 6, 2020).

Homework Assignment

**Review the information about impacts of incivility and write a
2000-word essay summarizing:**

a) In order of importance, which impacts (cost, customer retention,
    creativity, team spirit, trust, or performance) do you think are most
    relevant for manufacturing organizations and why?

Increased Costs

According to a study conducted by Accountemps and reported in Fortune,
managers and executives at Fortune 1,000 firms spend 13 percent of their

work time—the equivalent of seven weeks a year—mending employee relationships and otherwise dealing with the aftermath of incivility.[13]

HR research[14] shows incivility affects key business indicators. Nearly all (92 percent) Canadian HR professionals agree incivility has negative effects on productivity. Eighty percent report an impact on absenteeism. And 72 percent say customer service suffers as a result.[15]

U.S. academic research focusing on both Canadian and U.S. companies shows two out of three employees experienced a decline in performance after an incivility incident. Four out of five lost time worrying about the incident. And nearly half (47 percent) of the employees purposely lowered their effort or decreased their time at work due to incivility.[16]

A sample of costs that are associated with stress in the workplace[17]:

- 19 percent of absenteeism costs
- 40 percent of turnover costs
- 10 percent of drug plan costs
- 60 percent of workplace accidents
- 100 percent of stress-related lawsuits (e.g., *Bank of Montreal vs. Zorn-Smith, Honda, RCMP*) Chrysalis Performance Inc. Research

Negative Impact on Customer Retention

Public rudeness among employees is common, according to our survey of 244 consumers. Whether it is waiters berating fellow waiters or store clerks criticizing colleagues, disrespectful behavior makes people uncomfortable, and they are quick to walk out without making a purchase.[18]

---

[13]Accountemps. 2020. "#1 Accounting and Finance Staffing: Temporary Staffing You Can Count on." www.roberthalf.com/accountemps/free-resources (accessed April 3, 2020).

[14]S. Bar-David. n.d. "Benefits Column: Abrasive Employees Hurt Productivity," *BenefitsCanada.com*. www.benefitscanada.com/benefits/health-wellness/benefits-column-the-impact-of-workplace-incivility-62273 (accessed June 4, 2020).

[15]Ibid.

[16]Ibid.

[17]J. Burton. 2007. *Creating Healthy Workplaces* (Mississauga, ON: Industrial Accident Prevention Association).

[18]C. Porath, and C. Pearson. January–February 2013. "The Price of Incivility," *Harvard Business Review*. https://hbr.org/2013/01/the-price-of-incivility. 04/08/2019

Reduced Creativity and Innovation

Witnesses to rudeness also suffer a loss of cognitive powers and the ability to be creative, says a study[19] by Amir Erez, a psychologist at the University of Florida's school of management. It's just bad business, he says—one toxic employee can poison a whole office with a few angry outbursts and four-letter words.

"Managers should be very concerned because the negative consequences of rudeness on the job are not limited to the person who happens to be the victim," he said. "If five other people are watching, the effects are going to spill over into the rest of the organization." In an experiment Pearson and Porath conducted with Amir Erez, a professor of management at the University of Florida, participants who were treated rudely by other subjects were 30 percent less creative than others in the study. They produced 25 percent fewer ideas and the ones they did come up with were less original. For example, when asked what to do with a brick, participants who had been treated badly proposed logical but not particularly imaginative activities, such as "build a house," "build a wall," and "build a school." We saw more sparks from participants who had been treated civilly; their suggestions included "sell the brick on eBay," "use it as a goalpost for a street soccer game," "hang it on a museum wall and call it abstract art," and "decorate it like a pet and give it to a kid as a present."[20]

Performance and Team Spirit Deteriorate

Survey results and interviews indicate that simply witnessing incivility has negative consequences. In one experiment we conducted, people who had observed poor behavior performed 20 percent worse on word puzzles than other people did. We also found that witnesses to incivility were less likely than others to help out, even when the person they would be helping had no apparent connection to the uncivil person. Only 25 percent of

---

[19]Wharton Baker Retail. 2020. "Baker Retailing Center." https://bakerretail.wharton .upenn.edu/ (accessed March 2, 2020).

[20]C. Porath, and C. Pearson. January–February 2013. "The Price of Incivility," *Harvard Business Review*. https://hbr.org/2013/01/the-price-of-incivility. 05/06/2019

the subjects who had witnessed incivility volunteered to help, whereas 51 percent of those who hadn't witnessed it did.[21]

Reduced Trust and Disengagement

Nearly one in four of all employees suffer chronic anger on the job. Workplace anger is on the upswing, because people feel betrayed by their employer. One element of this perceived betray is constant uncertainty about the future of their jobs.[22]

Reduced Morale and Lower Productivity

Ralph Fevre, a professor of social research at Cardiff University said his research showed that incivility in the workplace translates into increased turnover, more sick days, lower morale, and poor productivity. But remedying this situation is not as straightforward as it would seem.

> Managers and supervisors are the single most important source of incivility in the workplace and some of this occurs as they pursue the objectives their employer has given them. This in turn suggests that companies sometimes lose sight of the fundamentals because they are determined to follow a particular strategy, Mr. Fevre said.

According to his research, incivility is most often demonstrated by shouting, insults, treating others disrespectfully, intimidating behavior, and persistent criticism. He said that there is a substantial overlap between incivility at work and other forms of ill-treatment in the workplace, including violence.

Naturally, some offices are worse than others but those that consider their work "super intense" are prone to problems of all types. The most reliable predictors of a troubled workplace? When employees feel they

---

[21]Ibid.

[22]S. Liptrap. March 4, 2020. "Improving Workplace Well-Being Sets Employees up for Success," *The Globe and Mail.* 04/05/2020www.theglobeandmail.com/business/careers/leadership/article-improving-workplace-well-being-sets-employees-up-for-success/.

need to compromise their principles or when organizations put their own needs ahead of their employees' well-being, Mr. Fevre said.[23]

Advanced Thinking—Preparing for Chapter 3

Over my 20+ years in the industry, I have experienced the typical manufacturing plant which would not be described as a nice place to work. While some of the people might be nice, some of the time, my experience has been that the workplace itself is often not very nice. Manufacturing can be dirty work under harsh conditions, tight timelines, constant change, and ever-increasing demands to do more with less. As a result, the overall tone of the environment is far from nice.

Maybe it's because manufacturing has traditionally been male-dominated, or because the work is perceived to be strenuous or physical and the conditions tough, that the tendency has been for leadership to be "rough" on their teams. By rough I mean, stereotypically "male"—no weak behavior tolerated; no crying, no touchy-feely nonsense, and no acting like you care about anything other than getting the job done. Basically no "nice" is expected or allowed. Nice is for the weak.

In traditional manufacturing environments, you need to show you are not weak. Fitting in often requires being "rough" which might include engaging in behaviors such as:

- Swearing
- Calling people names
- Ignoring people
- Criticizing people in public
- Walking away when people are talking to you
- Shouting
- Demonstrating physical strength, e.g., punching a wall, stomping, making a fist

---

[23]https://www.plymouth.ac.uk/uploads/production/document/path/11/11005/ Insight_report_Fevre__Lewis__Robinson_and_Jones.pdf, Insight into ill-treatment in the workplace: patterns, causes and solutions Ralph Fevre, Duncan Lewis, Amanda Robinson and Trevor Jones Published July 2011, 06/08/2019

- Toughing it out when you experience small injuries
- Crowding others, e.g., getting into their personal space
- Overtalking and/or interrupting
- Rolling your eyes
- Gesturing rudely, e.g., giving the finger
- Shutting people down verbally
- Speaking in a harsh tone
- Taking staunch stance, e.g., wide postures
- Failing to acknowledge others
- Avoiding showing softness, e.g., formal thank you, hugging, too much smiling
- Avoiding apologizing

And generally, just not being nice.

As a result of this "be strong to survive" mindset, manufacturing plants are not perceived as great places to work. Sure the noise, the time constraints, the stress, the union aspects, etc. all contribute to what can be described as a toxic workplace culture, but mostly, the lack of niceness is due to leadership (including supervisors and managers) and their respective attitudes toward what constitutes acceptable "people treatment." People treatment is a civility term that refers to an overall attitude about what constitutes a fair and good way of interacting with people. It includes how you speak, nonverbal gestures, the extent to which you are empathetic, and how you define honesty and integrity.

When I trained to be a Master Civility Trainer, one of the key messages I took away is that civility is a choice. Most of us know what is right and wrong, but with regard to people treatment, "[...] good people sometimes make bad decisions about how to treat others due in large part to relinquishing their personal power to others, or due to perceived expectations or pressure in specific environments."[24] Lew suggests that people treatment is a complex dynamic, but basically nurture—workplace culture in this case—rather than nature—the personal traits and qualities of the individuals in the culture—defines

---

[24]Lew Bayer. CEO, Civility Experts Inc. 2019

decision-making, especially related to interpersonal relationships and people treatment. I believe this may be true of many manufacturing environments, and it was in fact true of several organizations where I worked.

Clearly it is time for change, but is it possible to change behavior and mindset in workplace cultures where toxicity and incivility are a habit, and/or encouraged?

What do you think?

CHAPTER 3

Changing Workplace Culture

A corporation is a living organism; it has to continue to shed its skin. Methods have to change. Focus has to change. Values have to change. The sum of those changes is transformation.

—Andrew Grove

As discussed in Chapter 1, there are those in the manufacturing industry who would argue that the **workplace culture** "is what it is." They might suggest that the work gets done, and that command and control management achieves, and sometimes surpasses, the organizational goals. The fact is, the industry has survived for a long time, changing when necessary, in terms of technology, and regulations, and even safety. There have been quality improvements and the industry thrives in many countries around the world.

The conversation is no different than in other sectors when there is resistance to change—those who are comfortable with how it has always been done, stay, and those who don't like the culture find their way out of it, one way or another.

For the purposes of this book, our focus is not on changing processes specifically—unless those processes tie into workplace communication. Our focus will be sharing strategies for building trust, engaging in civil communication, encouraging collaboration, fostering information sharing, embedding a culture of learning, and increasing morale. Our field experience suggests that these factors have a significant impact on employees' overall experience in the workplace.

Still, for the record, we do know from the research (e.g., Weber Shadwick) that when an organization can incorporate civility as best practice, including embedding it in aspects of policy, procedure, and process as well as in communication protocols, and when leaders adopt the mindset that civility in and of itself is a **continuous improvement** strategy, organizations can experience additional, and measurable, improvements to retention, engagement, and to productivity, among other metrics.

So, what do we mean by "workplace culture"? There are many theories and definitions about what workplace culture is but we (Bayer & Masotti) define workplace culture as "the habits, traditions, attitudes, tone of interactions, and general behaviors that make up employees' day-to-day experience." An individual experiences workplace culture by living in the workplace. And because we typically interact with, and impact, those we work with, the people living in an organization co-create the workplace culture.

When we understand workplace culture in this way, it is easy to also understand how, in the words of Scott Peck, in *A World Waiting to be Born*, that genuine "civility is part consciously motivated organizational behaviour." Scott suggests that this is because civility has to do with how we relate to each other, and whenever there is a relationship between two or more people, an organization of some sort is involved. In manufacturing this is true; for example, production teams might interact with supervisors and union representatives (an organization) who in turn interact with managers who may interact with a regulating body (an organization) or with a supplier (an organization) or with a customer (an organization) and so on.

One of the mistakes many organizations make when they set out to change workplace culture, especially if the focus is on people treatment, is thinking short-term. Often when people behave badly, training is identified as the solution, for example, teach people how to communicate, or offer **respectful workplace** or **emotional intelligence** and managing conflict and diversity training. In some cases, there might be some positive impact of these training solutions but frequently there is not. The reasons training in and of itself is not enough to change workplace culture are:

- The specific skills, knowledge, and abilities needed are not properly assessed; e.g., the work team is simply sent to and required to attend all generic training.

- The employees often do not understand why they are attending training and they don't know what they are expected to do with what they learn—*if* they learn something.
- The training is not linked to goals, policy, procedure, etc.
- There is no follow-up or evaluation—no testing, rewards, or consequences for doing anything (or nothing) with the learning.

This is why civility training is usually only effective when it is one part of a bigger change initiative.

What is a **change initiative?** As presented in Chapter 2, building a culture of civility in a manufacturing organization where what we may perceive as a toxic culture has prevailed for, in some cases, a hundred years, might be a difficult endeavor. It's not going to be easy to change the workplace culture, and it is likely not going to happen quickly. As such, this type of change is best handled as a change initiative. To be successful, leaders and organizations must understand and acknowledge that there is more to civility as a continuous improvement strategy than simply offering civility training.

A change initiative is usually a companywide mandate that supports changes required to meet organizational goals. Change isn't easy.

IMPORTANT: Gallup polls assert that 70 percent of all change initiatives fail because change agents overlook the role frontline supervisors and managers play in the success of the initiative. They also claim that HR professionals fail to develop in frontline managers the exact skills and actions they need to take to make the changes happen.

Other reasons why change initiatives fail include:

- The lack of a clearly communicated strategy to stakeholders such as employees and customers
- The lack of support and buy-in by key organizational leaders; even if the change initiative is small in scope, senior leaders must be aware of it, understand why it is important to the organization as a whole, and "own" it as if the decision is in the best interests of their own employees.
- Senior leaders' failure to understand the change initiative's relevance and the failure to measure the change initiative's progress
- The lack of sufficient technology to implement and sustain the change initiative

- The lack of positive and transparent reinforcement
- A lack of understanding about how the change will actually impact employees,[1] and the resulting organizational behaviour

Organizational behaviour is the study of how human beings behave in organizations. This field of study in the broadest sense covers most of human psychology, since human behavior occurs in the context of one or more organizations.

For Consideration: Civility Indicators Iceberg

The nuances and rationale for various aspects of workplace culture are not always obvious, and so in order to change workplace culture you have to look beyond what you can see and hear. One way of looking at workplace culture is imagining an iceberg. Over the course of a typical day, we observe or experience what is on the surface—the tip of the iceberg.

As a point of interest, the civility indicator iceberg is an adaptation of the original iceberg model, also called the **theory of omission** by Ernest Hemingway. The theory is that we cannot see or detect most of a situation's data. Hemingway used the model in his writing in that he deliberately only wrote about the "surface" of a scenario. Hemingway was a skilled enough writer that the reader speculated or devised what was under the surface. He intentionally wrote so that what was beneath the surface was implicit. The model is now frequently used in understanding systems and in problem-solving.

Consider again, the "tip of the iceberg" in a workplace. As depicted in the civility indicator iceberg graphic, we can see:

- How people dress
- How people interact, including with whom, and how
- The tone of communications, e.g., harsh, or friendly

---

[1]UNC Executive Development. November 12, 2015. "Why Change Initiatives Fail," *Executive Development Blog.* http://execdev.kenan-flagler.unc.edu/blog/why-change-initiatives-fail#:~:text=The%20lack%20of%20sufficient%20technology,change%20 will%20actually%20impact%20employees, (accessed August 14, 2020).

- What cliques or clusters or hierarchy exist
- What the people who work in the organization do, e.g., tasks, roles
- Who the people who work in an organization are, e.g., age, race, gender, education, experience, language
- What gets done, e.g., errors, production, safety measures
- The general demeanor or mood of the workplace, e.g., stressful, happy, supportive, etc.
- Overall standards, e.g., is the workplace clean, organized, structured
- Other

The problem with only seeing what is above the surface is that this purview rarely helps us understand WHY things are the way they are above the surface. When we look below the surface, we can begin to understand factors that influence, direct, or dictate what happens day-to-day. For example:

- Legislation/regulation
- Organizational policy
- Process and procedures
- Financial situation, e.g., resources for repairs or training
- External conditions, e.g., recession
- Demographics, e.g., labor pool
- Competencies, e.g., of leadership team
- Stakeholder interests, e.g., union
- Compliance expectations
- History, e.g., no competitors, no enforcement of safety standards, poor quality control
- Habits, history, and patterns in terms of hierarchy, communication expectations, and approach
- Relationships and power distribution
- Management style/approach
- Other, e.g., the trends, world events, discoveries, inventions, and other influences that impact our world and how we work every day

The reality is that long-standing policies and practices, sometimes even processes and procedures, can actually encourage incivility. While these processes may seem logical or can be rationalized as necessary due to

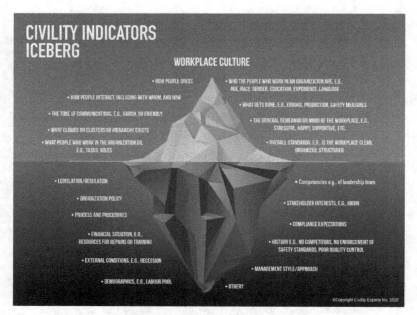

Figure 4 Civility Indicators Iceberg©, Civility Experts Inc. 2018

financial priorities and other reasons, the impact relative to **"people treat-ment"** and the overall employee experience is downplayed or overlooked.

The bottom line is, if you want to change workplace culture, you have to change the day-to-day experience of the employees. And this means being open and honest to really looking at how people are being treated. In addition, as leaders, you have to be open to criticism and take respon-sibility for your contribution to the day-to-day experience of those you work with. And, you have to be change-ready. You have to be willing and competent to make the necessary changes to your own attitudes and behavior such that you can contribute in a positive way to employees' day-to-day life in the organization.

As an aside, a recent Change Lab 2019 Workplace Survey found that it's not the pace of change in workplaces that is wearing people down or burning them out. It's how leaders approach change and how successful the changes are that either causes workers to thrive or to barely get by. The sur-vey also showed that it's not the ability of leaders to tell-and-control that de-livers the best change results. Instead, it's their ability to invite-and-inquire as they bring diverse voices into meaningful change conversations and give them the freedom to self-organize and take action.

And, according to Shirish Jain, Lead Consultant, Transformation Management with Larsen & Toubro Group,

[...] managing change in the manufacturing industry can get much more complex than expected, when compared with other industries, particularly when it comes to handling change for people working on the shop floor. They have a highly focused thought process, a way of working and any change that transforms their day-to-day work is dealt with strong resistance. It gets complicated further due to strong unions that push the change back. The change is perceived differently by different stakeholders. While shop-floor workers will be worried about potential job losses due to automation and a steep learning curve for latest technology adoption, the management faces a challenge of huge manufacturing skill gap and how to upskill relatively older generation employees who are not tech savvy. Increasing regulatory and compliance measures associated with technology changes, is another critical aspect organizations deal with.

Shirish goes on to recommend focus in five areas to manage the people side of change. These are listed below with some questions I would ask you to consider.

- Effective sponsorship—Establishing a strong sponsorship network by leveraging influential stakeholders in various departments
  ○ *THINK ABOUT IT: How do you establish "strong" sponsorship? And what does "strong" mean? What does it look like? Isn't this about trust and engagement?*
- Unified communication—In manufacturing, various departments are often reliant on one another to get the job done. Hence, the necessity of frequent and timely communication to other teams when an action has been performed, is highly imperative.
  ○ *THINK ABOUT IT: How do you encourage cross-team communication? And how do you communicate effectively? For example, it's fine to say we need to do these things, but people*

don't know how. Or, sometimes the process and situational factors actually inhibit communication.

- Coaching—Time to time coaching is essential for managing any resistance coming through strong unions' demands. There needs to be focused discussions and workshops planned to communicate about the change.
  - *THINK ABOUT IT: What is coaching? Do supervisors and managers have coaching skills? How do you coach in time-strained environments? And why are we only coaching during periods of resistance?*
- Training—With fast-evolving technology changes in the manufacturing sector, there is a need to prepare the next generation of the workforce, which is skilled and more adaptive to changes.
  - *THINK ABOUT IT: What if the workforce does not have continuous learning skills? What if skills are not being assessed properly? How do you know training is effective?*
- Change sustenance—In order to sustain the change, there should be a constant feedback loop and on-the-go course correction by key stakeholders. From the stakeholder perspective, there must be representation from all the key functions, including HR teams, when it comes to change in any work-related policies or behavior.
  - *THINK ABOUT IT: Who is giving the feedback? How are they giving feedback?*

While all of this makes sense on the surface, as per the bold sections above, it is not enough to determine "*what*" should happen to manage change. When it comes to managing people during change, the "*how*" is significantly more important. And the reality is, when civility is embedded into the workplace as common practice, that is, supervisors and managers learn how to show respect and how to communicate in a civil way every day, in every interaction, and when the organization adopts civility policies related to transparency, fair play, ethics, etc., the fact is, change of any kind is less difficult.

In the Advanced Thinking section of Chapter 2, I suggested that most of us know what is right and wrong, but with regard to people treatment, "[…] good people sometimes make bad decisions about how to treat others due in large part to relinquishing their personal power to others, or due to perceived expectations or pressure in specific environments."[2] Lew suggests that people treatment is a complex dynamic, but basically nurture—workplace culture in this case—rather than nature—the personal traits and qualities of the individuals in the culture, defines decision-making, especially related to interpersonal relationships and people treatment. I believe this may be true of many manufacturing environments, and it was in fact true of several organizations where I worked.

Question

Using the iceberg metaphor, draw an iceberg showing what might be below the surface for each of the following behaviors which would be observed in a manufacturing environment.

Scenario 1

Decision-making—Observed above the surface:

- Silence
- Eye-rolling
- Shrugging shoulders
- Disengagement

Scenario 2

Errors—Observed above the surface:

- Employee appears to have correct equipment.
- Employee appears to know what to do.
- Employee continually makes unacceptable errors.

---

[2]Lew Bayer. CEO Civility Experts Inc. 2016

Scenario 3

Failure to wear safety equipment (personal protection equipment)—Observed on the surface:

- Requirements are in the employee handbook.
- Other employees on the team are wearing PPE.
- Supervisor has asked employee to put PPE on.
- Employee has been provided with the equipment.

Addressing the people side of change is an important aspect of ensuring a successful change initiative. Sadly, this is the piece that many organizations fail to acknowledge and/or plan for.

Based on 20 years of fieldwork designing and implementing workplace civility initiatives combined with 20 years of workplace experience, we (Bayer & Masotti) have collaborated to devise a workplace civility initiative strategy called "The Trident Approach."

The Trident Approach® (Masotti & Bayer) to Changing Workplace Culture

The Trident Approach is a three-step approach to changing workplace culture. The approach presents as an "initiative" in that it goes beyond merely offering training and instead addresses multiple aspects of the organization's framework.

Specifically, the Trident Approach:

- Incorporates targeted, customized, civility training as a requirement for any or all leadership roles
- Embeds civility in human resources processes and as such represents a meaningful and strategic continuous improvement strategy that supports:
  - skills development and performance
  - trust and engagement
  - continuous learning
  - positive workplace experience/culture

In addition, the approach includes specific civility-focused leadership skills and knowledge for:

- Introducing and implementing SOPs
- Assessing skills
- Conducting on-the-job coaching including giving feedback
- Problem-solving
- Removing perceived performance barriers

There are three "prongs" to the approach:

- Targeted civility-focused communication training
- A strategic technique for observation and assessment
- Application of the "Masotti Methods" which include specific ways of:
  - Observing and gathering information
  - Giving feedback
  - Reducing variability

Step 1: Teaches leaders the value and impact of civility and incorporates key learnings about "how" to engage in civil communication, e.g., incorporating civility into tone, word choice, and demeanor. The strategy incorporates social intelligence aspects including social radar, social style, and

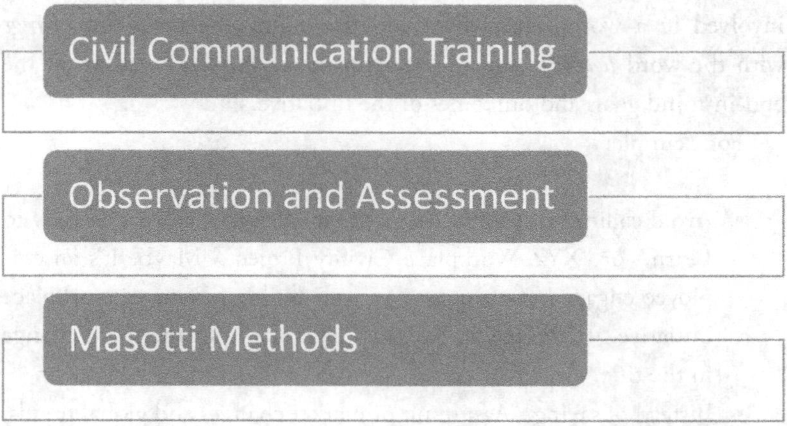

Civil Communication Training

Observation and Assessment

Masotti Methods

Figure 5 The Trident©, Masotti, 2019

social knowledge. Ideally this training happens BEFORE the change initiative is introduced.

Step 2: Observe and assess the current situation, culture, and practices, e.g., use the civility culture continuum, civility symptoms survey, change readiness and trust assessments, skills and competency testing, etc., as well as the signature AEIOU® method to understand the current situation and identify priority needs. Ideally assessment and observation happen before, and throughout the change initiative.

Step 3: Apply "The Masotti Methods." The signature Masotti methodology includes two specific models that support steps 1 and 2 of the Trident and teach supervisors/managers how to give feedback, and how to fix any people-oriented problems that are not resolved through civility best practices, e.g., via the Masotti feedback method, or the "make the box smaller process" for reducing **variability**. Ideally the Masotti methods are applied both during and after the change initiative is implemented.

As an aside, and as one way of subtly incorporating civility into workplace culture, consider teaching leaders not to use the word "change." Since many people have a visceral reaction and assume the worst when they hear the word "change," it is recommended to encourage everyone involved in a workplace civility initiative to replace the word *change* with the word *learning* and to focus on the positive, as well as on the end-in-mind goals and outcomes of the initiative.

For example:

- Avoid calling your initiative a change initiative, call it a "Ready to Learn," or "XYZ Workplace Civility Project." Maybe it's an employee engagement program or your building a better workplace initiative, whatever you like; just try not to put the word change in the title.
- Instead of saying, "As a result of market changes and global trends, we all have to change. We need to work faster and be more agile,"

say, "We can build on our current skills and take this opportunity to learn as we adapt to trends and market shifts."

- Don't say, "You need to change how you work," say, "Learning how to work differently will make you more efficient."

- Rather than saying, "You are all required to attend change management training," say, "The continuous learning course we're all taking, is going to help us manage whatever comes our way."

- Employees are more inclined to get excited about learning opportunities versus requirements to change, and people usually like knowing what the benefit of the change/learning will be. For example, say, "We can all reduce our daily stress by learning how to manage our time better. Attendance requested: Learning opportunity for supervisors, every Tuesday 9–11 a.m.," versus saying, "We are wasting too much time and must do things differently. Mandatory training for supervisors. Time management training six consecutive Tuesday mornings 9–11 a.m."

The Trident Approach offers a way of problem-solving without leaders even realizing they are problem-solving. For example, incorporating civility training prior to issues or changes occurring sets leaders and teams up for success when issues and questions and challenges arise.

And civility is easy to teach on the job. Because civility is about people treatment, supervisors and managers can be taught how to behave civilly in a relatively short time. And they in turn can then teach others just by leading by example. Civility is difficult to understand if a person doesn't experience it, and so the quickest and easiest way to coach and teach civility is to simply ask supervisors and managers to "live it"—that is, behave in a civil way and consistently engage in positive people treatment. When the employee team experiences the impact of this positive treatment, they naturally want the positive treatment to continue and so they often mirror the overall tone and approach of their civil higher-ups and a reciprocal relationship starts to develop.

A key outcome of this reciprocity is high trust among and across the work team at all levels. When this high trust is established when things are going well—just because it is a way of being and living in the culture that is expected and endorsed—the trust is carried through to stressful situations. Because there is high **trust**, it tends to be easier for teams to work together through issues and crises. This is because trust fosters increased:

- communication
- support, e.g., help with tasks, mentoring, empathy
- personal responsibility
- understanding of accountability to the team
- wellness, e.g., due to less stress
- sharing and collaboration
- ability for teams to accept decisions and changes without fear and worry
- engagement

Civility training is like stocking the shelf or assembling a toolbox. It prepares people for what might come next. When you use the Trident Approach, you can eliminate **kaizen** and meetings and wasted time. This is because the majority of what is perceived as "problems," e.g., people being late, people not doing what they're told, people not being happy at work, are largely due to negative people treatment. If you teach leaders how to treat people well, people will typically perform better. And they will perform better as a habit versus as a requirement. This makes civility a preemptive, proactive problem-solving strategy.

See Chapter 9 for Optional Assignment.

Words to Know

- Workplace culture
- Continuous improvement
- Respectful workplace
- Emotional intelligence
- Change initiative
- Organizational behaviour
- Theory of omission
- People treatment
- Personal protective equipment (PPE)

- Trust
- Kaizen
- Variability

For Review

As explained earlier in the chapter, one of the key requirements for a successful change initiative is high trust. And one of the ways you can build trust is by teaching supervisors and managers to lead with civility. By exhibiting civil communication and related positive people treatment, employees' day-to-day experience living in the workplace can change in a meaningful and positive way.

Here are three situations/scenarios where leaders have an opportunity to build trust and a list of specific behaviors for doing so.

Scenario #1: Vacation Planning

I have found that for many production employees, one of the most important aspects of feeling in control on the job (besides safety) is their availability to book vacations. Factors important for building trust in this scenario include transparency and sharing information. Specifically, leaders can do the following:

- Let the employee know exactly how much vacation he or she is allowed.
- Let the person know if it is mandatory for vacations to be booked during shutdowns and holidays like Christmas time.
- Be transparent and have a chart or readily available information (like a posted chart of what days are available and what days are booked already).
- Have a standardized process for booking vacations—a formula; For example, seniority, job class, skills coverage.
- Make it clear that the vacation is to be planned and booked far in advance.
- Leave a buffer for emergency days.
- Collect data and discover patterns in absence days or shifts and plan manpower and vacations accordingly.

By collecting data and being transparent with posted information, the process becomes less emotional, and most of the decisions are made by the employee based on transparent information before his or her request gets made.

- This streamlines the vacation booking process and employees feel more comfortable and less stressed when booking vacations. Employees see the effort you are putting in to ease their experience at work and this builds trust.

Scenario #2: Mis-Build or Mistakes on the Job

In my experience, when an employee makes a mistake at work, you can use this as an opportunity to build trust with the employee by doing the following:

- Look at the process and how that process allowed the employee to make a mistake.
- Focus on the process and not on the individual who made the mistake.
- Involve the employee with questions about the process, versus asking questions directed to the person. For example, ask, "How long does it typically take to run the cycle?" instead of "Why are you taking 52 minutes to run the cycle?"
- Ask if the employee has been trained. Ask when that training took place. Ask who delivered the training. And ask if the employee needs more training.
- Ensure that the employee has the right tools or skills to perform the job.
- Ask if the employee has any suggestions to improve the job.
- Ask if the employee has ever suggested improvements.
- If yes, ask more questions. What were the suggestions? Did they ever get acted upon? Was it a success? Where you thanked for the suggestion?
- If no, ask the employee why he or she has never made a suggestion.

- Provide corrective actions and plan on all answers. Give timelines on when you will get back to employee. Follow up with results within those timelines.
- Give results of the suggestions within timelines.
- Give answers if not all suggestions could be acted upon.
- Explain that not all suggestions can be acted upon based on timelines, ordering parts or supplies, changing collective agreement, and costs.
- Be open and give all information you can. If some answers cannot be given due to confidential information, then be honest and say so.

By investigating an employee's mistake and looking at the process and not the individual, the employee will be more comfortable giving information to improve his or her work.

- Trust is revealed when employees offer information and this process is key because it is PROACTIVE and prevents mistakes in the future.
- This circle of trust and release of information is the most important aspect of continuous improvement, and civility of this process is the precursor.

Scenario #3: Requests for Tools or Supplies from a Person to Do a Job

One thing I learned early on is that the biggest opportunities to gain trust are the requests you can respond to immediately.

- A good example would be requests for items like PPE, safety glasses, gloves, wrist guards, or a boot slip to get new safety boots. Get these items as soon as possible so the employee knows that he or she can rely on you to complete simple requests.
- More complex requests like tools require due diligence. Items like a new battery gun, replacement of worn sockets bits, etc., customized tools specific to an operation, or any item that cannot be delivered immediately require your due diligence to acquire and you

should state so, and keep the employee updated on progress resolving the request.

- Your due diligence needs to be transparent. Give feedback and follow up on what you are doing to get the tools and the timelines on when and if they will arrive. If the request cannot be delivered, be up-front and tell the employee why.

Trust is built when your employees' simple requests are addressed immediately or at least in a timely manner. Requests that will take longer to complete require your due diligence and you should mention this to the employee. Being transparent and including the employee in the details about the response to the request will help the employee feel confident that you are following through. He or she will also feel more sure that you care about the suggestion and that you value him or her as a person with something to contribute.

How Much Do You Remember?

1. According to Gallup, what percentage of change initiatives fail?
   a. 35 percent
   b. 62 percent
   c. 70 percent
   d. 90 percent
2. The iceberg theory is sometimes called what?
   a. The theory of everything
   b. The theory of omission
   c. Hemmingway method
   d. Surface theory
3. According to Masotti & Bayer, workplace culture is "the habits, traditions, attitudes, tone of interactions, and general behaviors that make up employees' day-to-day experience." True or False?
4. In order of application, the three prongs in the Masotti Trident Approach are:
   a. Assessment, training, feedback
   b. Evaluation, training, feedback
   c. Training, assessment, feedback
   d. Feedback, assessment, training

Recommended Reading

Bruno, B. 2017. *Change in Manufacturing.* Scotts Valley, CA: CreateSpace.

Homework Assignment

Review the chart below depicting the Workplace Incivility Filtering System. Choose one of the examples of a symptom of incivility (shown in the octagon at the top of the chart) and then write an explanation of how you could apply the filtering system to address that problem. For example:

a. Re: the first "filter of civility" how specifically would you:
    - Build trust?
    - Identify skills gaps that might be causing the symptom?
    - Identify how eliminating that incivility symptom would align with an organizational goal?
    - Address aspects of change resistance and/or readiness potentially related to that symptom?
    - What specific training would you provide to address the skills gap identified?
    - How would you communicate the expectations for alternative behaviors, e.g., to replace the incivility symptom?
b. Describe some potential observations. For example, once you have completed the actions related to a) above, what potential challenges, issues, or outcomes might you observe?
c. Once you assess, adjust, and measure (filter) until the incivility is resolved, explain which measurable metric might be most impacted.

Advanced Thinking—Preparing for Chapter 4

In my experience, many of the problems that teams are tasked with solving, the projects that they spend time and money on, would not even have arisen as problems if civility had been embedded into the organization's policies and practices. Examples of this are "low-hanging fruit" problems that often take up many of the resources allocated to continuous improvement, and sadly do not always show good return on investment or long-term benefits.

What do you think?

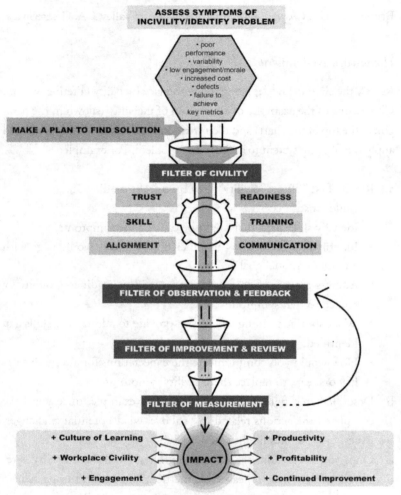

Figure 6 Workplace Incivility Filtering System©, Masotti, 2019

CHAPTER 4

Civility as a Continuous Improvement Strategy

An environment where people have to think brings with it wisdom, and this wisdom brings with it kaizen [continuous improvement].
—Teruyuki Minoura

As discussed in Chapter 3, the **Trident Approach®** is an intervention strategy for changing workplace culture via behavior and mindset shifts. The first prong of the trident is civility training. Civility training offers skill-building in positive people treatment as a preventative step that potentially offsets the need for:

- Wasting time and/or resources on people-oriented problems, e.g., including these issues as continuous improvement projects. This is because when individuals practice civility, much of these day-to-day issues resolve themselves. Examples of this are behaviors that relate to sharing information, asking questions, taking personal responsibility, following basic rules, self-directing learning, etc.
- Engaging in generic, "flavor of the month" training or training for the sake of training. Instead, at a fraction of the cost, organizations can teach four core skills that enable civil behavior and concurrently address many other skill gaps.
- The four core skills that underpin the ability to be civil at work are:
  - **Continuous learning**—fosters self-directed learning, supports knowledge workers, and promotes change readiness.

- ○ **Systems thinking**—helps individuals see their place, power, and impact relative to the system they are in and the systems they interact with. Systems thinking fosters confidence, trust, and problem-solving.
- ○ **Social intelligence**—enables individuals to read verbal, nonverbal, tonal, and contextual cues and to interpret them effectively. This helps them anticipate, adapt, and repair their approach and behavior appropriately. Social intelligence includes social radar, social knowledge, and social style.
- ○ **Cultural competence**—This skill encompasses both organizational culture and heritage cultural competence. This ability supports working in teams, understanding differences that make a difference, recognizing where process overrides preference, and generally helps promote respect at work.
- Constantly having to manage interpersonal issues related to miscommunication and uncivil tone and approach to conversations. When employees and leaders respect themselves and each other, there are significantly less interpersonal and miscommunication issues to deal with.
- Planning training in topic areas such as those below because, when done well, civility training incorporates the four underpinning skills that support all of these add-on topics. This saves training dollars and reduces time off the floor.
  - ○ Diversity
  - ○ Teamwork
  - ○ Conflict management
  - ○ General communication
  - ○ Change management
  - ○ Emotional intelligence
  - ○ Building trust
  - ○ Working with various generations
  - ○ Collaboration

Clearly, there is a solid business case for offering your teams civility training. (We get into the specifics of what to train, and who, in Chapter 5). Once organizations understand that civility is a measurable competency that manifests in part through the expression of advanced "soft skills," they tend to take it more seriously.

This is a good thing, as research carried out by the Carnegie Institute of Technology shows that 85 percent of your financial success is due to skills in "human engineering," your personality and ability to communicate, negotiate, and lead. Shockingly, only 15 percent is due to technical knowledge.[1]

Dr. John Fleenor of the Center for Creative Leadership explains that the CEO's **"soft skills"** make all the difference. To be successful, individuals must be good listeners, consensus builders, team players, and empathizers. Hence, to climb the corporate ladder quickly, it is essential for executives to possess more soft skills and less hard skills. We can compare soft skills with emotional intelligence quotient (EQ) and hard skills with intelligence quotient (IQ). Succinctly, soft skills are twice as important as IQ or technical skills for the success of senior executives. Studies have shown that individuals with a high emotional quotient are highly appreciated in the workplace and they tend to grow rapidly in the corporate chain.[2]

Daniel Goleman, author of several books on relational intelligence, says that soft skills are a combination of competencies that contribute to a person's ability to manage him or herself and relate to other people. These are the skills, abilities, and traits about the personality, attitude, and behavior of a person. They are the human skills that make a huge difference to your professional success. They are needed for good leaders to become great leaders. In contrast, hard skills are about your technical competence and domain expertise. Sometimes soft skills are equated with teamwork, while hard skills with execution. Hence, executives must proportionately blend their soft and hard skills with leadership to excel as successful leaders. However, as they gain more experience they need more soft skills because they work less on their hard skills and more on interpersonal skills.

---

[1]**Intelligence Is Overrated: What You Really Need To Succeed,** ." 2012. https://www.forbes.com/sites/keldjensen/2012/04/12/intelligence-is-overrated-what-you-really-need-to-succeed/#4b0ea0c5b6d2 08/30/2020

[2]Leading Effectively Staff. n.d. "Press Releases Archives," *Center for Creative Leadership*. www.ccl.org/leadership/news/2002/softskillssurvey.aspx?pageId=694 (accessed June 4, 2020).

They are mostly into visioning, troubleshooting, and managing several stakeholders which demands soft skills and leadership skills.[3]

In addition, Nobel Prize winning psychologist Daniel Kahneman found that people would rather do business with a person they like and trust rather than someone they don't, even if the person they don't like is offering a better price or higher quality product.[4] The ability to build trust is largely based on soft skills.

The benefits of individual leaders and employees building their civility competency in and of itself can change workplace culture. But the longer-lasting culture transformation happens when civility training is treated as one piece of an overall workplace civility initiative.

As a companywide initiative, civility would become embedded in:

- Company values
- Company mission
- Policies, e.g., expanded respectful workplace, discipline, language at work, etc.
- Processes, e.g., recruiting, hiring, promoting, incentive
- Training plan, specifically civility training would be mandatory and one of the first topics addressed, maybe second to safety
- Practices, e.g., how people are coached, feedback, written communications, etc.

Generally, in a civil workplace, employees are more likely to:

- Show consideration for each other
- Support their supervisors and managers
- Encourage positive interaction between union and management
- Seek solutions versus identify problems
- Be responsible for themselves, e.g., not make excuses for not meeting general expectations such as being on time, dressing appropriately, following basic rules, etc.

---

[3]M. Wilson. March 10, 2014. "Acquire Soft Skills to Fast-Track Your Career Success," *Under30CEO*. http://under30ceo.com/acquire-soft-skills-fast-track-career-success/.
[4]D. Kahneman. 2015. *Thinking, Fast and Slow* (New York, NY: Farrar, Straus and Giroux).

However, when civility is a core value and becomes a part of the character of the company, civility becomes a game-changing continuous improvement strategy with measurable results. This is true for organizations across sectors and the impacts are broad and varied. These include:

Profitability

- Companies that openly promote civil communication among employees earn 30 percent more revenue than competitors.[5]

Increased Revenue and Engagement

- Companies that openly promote civil communication among employees are four times more likely to have highly engaged employees, and are 20 percent more likely to report reduced turnover (Watson Wyatt Civility Survey).[6]
- In addition to skills gains, program participants in the UpSkills— Essentials to Excel (focused on Essential Skills for Hospitality) conducted by the Social Research and Demonstration Corporation, experienced significant improvements in job performance that were accompanied by a number of positive effects for businesses. A greater breadth of service quality and improved relations with customers were observed, leading to increased customer loyalty, repeat sales, and higher revenues. Increased task efficiency and accuracy led to fewer errors and lower costs of supervision. Ultimately, improved performance was accompanied by greater job retention, leading to higher earnings for employees and lower turnover costs for employers.[7]

---

[5]W. Shandwick, and P. Tate. 2011. "Civility in America 2011." www.webershandwick.com/uploads/news/files/Civility_in_America_2011.pdf.

[6]Willis Towers Watson. n.d. "Location Selector." www.towerswatson.com.

[7]The Social Research and Demonstration Corporation. August 18, 2014. "New Study Shows Net Benefits of Essential Skills Training in the Workplace." www.srdc.org/news/new-study-shows-net-benefits-of-essential-skills-training-in-the-workplace.aspx.

Increased Morale, Physical and Mental Health, and Happiness at Work

- Half of all employees who say that they do not feel valued at work report that they intend to look for a new job in the next year according to a survey by the American Psychological Association (APA). Conducted online among 1,714 adults between January 12 and 19, 2012 on behalf of the APA by Harris Interactive, the survey found that employees who feel valued are more likely to report better physical and mental health, as well as higher levels of engagement, satisfaction and motivation, compared to those who do not feel valued by their employers.

- Almost all employees (93 percent) who reported feeling valued said that they are motivated to do their best at work and 88 percent reported feeling engagedIn a Civility, Respect, and Engagement in the Workplace (CREW) intervention, a 6-month process that fosters civil interactions between employees, participants in the intervention experienced increases in civility with decreases in workplace distress and incivility after completing CREW. These improvements continued to increase one year after the intervention ended.[8]

Increased Performance and Productivity

- The greatest differentiators in performance and achievement are "soft skills" and mindset. Recent scientific studies have established that positive intelligence (PQ) is a significant determinant of how much of your potential for both happiness and professional success you actually achieve. Positive intelligence has been directly linked to a wide range of measurable benefits[9]:
  - Salespeople sell 37 percent more.

---

[8]M.P. Leiter, A. Day, D.G. Oore, and H.K.S. Laschinger. 2012. "Getting Better and Staying Ber: Assessing Civility, Incivility, Distress, and Job Attitudes One Year after a Civility Intervention," *Journal of Occupational Health Psychology* 17, no. 4, pp. 425-434.

[9]Positive Intelligence. n.d. "Saboteurs." http://positiveintelligence.com/overview/science/.

- ○ Teams perform 31 percent better with high-PQ leaders.
- ○ Creative output increases 3×.
- ○ People live as much as 10 years longer.
- A study of workplace hiring practices by L'Oreal showed that salespeople hired based on their emotional intelligence made $90,000 more annually than those hired through traditional methods.[10]
- Behaviors involving persistence, self-discipline, effort, and compliance are likely to increase individual worker effectiveness.[11]

Increased Team Orientation and Ability to Work Well with Others

- The high (emotionally intelligent) EI individual, relative to others, is less apt to engage in problem behaviors, and avoids self-destructive, negative behaviors such as smoking, excessive drinking, drug abuse, or violent episodes with others. The high EI person is more likely to have possessions of sentimental attachment around the home and to have more positive social interactions, particularly if the individual scored highly on emotional management. Such individuals may also be more adept at describing motivational goals, aims, and missions.[12]

Interestingly, employees who experience poor people treatment seem to know, and want, civility when they see it: 67 percent of employees who responded to a Civility in America poll said they believe there is a strong need for civility training.[13]

---

[10]J. Freedman. n.d. "The Business Case for Emotional Intelligence," *Academia.edu.* www.academia.edu/1293046/The_Business_Case_for_Emotional_Intelligence.

[11]D. Kunkel, and D. Davidson. 2014. "Taking the Good with the Bad: Measuring Civility and Incivility," *Journal of Organizational Culture, Communications and Conflict.* The DreamCatchers Group, LLC. www.questia.com/read/1G1-397579873/taking-the-good-with-the-bad-measuring-civility-and (accessed January 1, 2014).

[12]S.J. Lopez, J.T. Pedrotti, and C R. Snyder. 2019. *Positive Psychology: The Scientific and Practical Explorations of Human Strengths* (Thousand Oaks, CA: SAGE Publications, Inc).

[13]W. Shandwick, and P. Tate. 2011. "Civility in America 2011." www.webershandwick.com/uploads/news/files/Civility_in_America_2011.pdf.

For Consideration—Civility in Practice

As depicted in the *Civility in Practice Model©*, civility happens before, during, and after a workplace "event." An event could be a change, a crisis, a safety issue, etc. Civility, when embedded into everyday practice and policy is preventative versus reactive.

However, if civility is not incorporated into an organization as a preventative measure, there are still benefits of training after the fact. For example, in addition to teaching how to prevent incivility, civility training offers strategies for how to repair breeches in trust and **social capital** which may result when civility is not part of the "event" management process from the beginning.

At whichever point civility is incorporated, it becomes a "**continuous improvement**" strategy. However, the highest impact is achieved when organizations engage in ongoing, incremental, and proactive civility-oriented behaviors, e.g., civility as a comprehensive change initiative.

Generally, continuous improvement is understood to be a deliberate, planned (and sometimes strategic), ongoing effort to improve products, services, or processes. Continuous improvement practices are widely endorsed across manufacturing. The missing piece in most organizations is that they do NOT apply continuous improvement processes to the people aspect of the work.

The people aspect of work includes:

- Aspects of workplace culture, e.g., the overall mood or tone of a workplace
- Environment aspects, e.g., whether there is sufficient lighting, air flow etc. (aspects that impact people's moods)
- Communication protocols related to transparency, tone of communication, frequency, and courtesy in messaging, e.g., not just honing processes about "what" information is communicated but also "why"
- The extent to which people feel valued
- The frequency and nature of communications
- Basic "comforts," e.g., do people have proper equipment, do they feel safe, do they get breaks, are they paid fairly, etc.

- How supervisors and leaders give feedback
  - Honesty
  - Equality
  - Equity
  - Integrity
- How the organization supports a culture of learning
- Incentive and reward programs
- The extent to which employees can fully engage, e.g., buy in to the organizational values and mission
- The extent of opportunities for growth, both personal and professional
- The extent to which employees feel pride, e.g., in their contribution, towards their team, about the organization's status in the community etc.

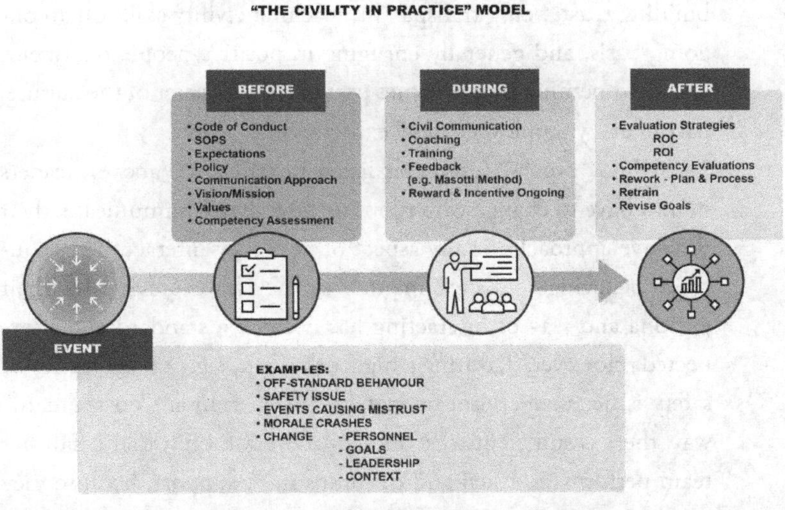

"THE CIVILITY IN PRACTICE" MODEL

BEFORE	DURING	AFTER

• Code of Conduct
• SOPS
• Expectations
• Policy
• Communication Approach
• Vision/Mission
• Values
• Competency Assessment
	• Civil Communication
	• Coaching
	• Training
	• Feedback
	  (e.g. Masotti Method)
	• Reward & Incentive Ongoing
		• Evaluation Strategies
		  ROC
		  ROI
		• Competency Evaluations
		• Rework - Plan & Process
		• Retrain
		• Revise Goals

EVENT

EXAMPLES:
- OFF-STANDARD BEHAVIOUR
- SAFETY ISSUE
- EVENTS CAUSING MISTRUST
- MORALE CRASHES
- CHANGE   - PERSONNEL
              - GOALS
              - LEADERSHIP
              - CONTEXT

Figure 7 Civility in Practice Model©, Masotti & Bayer 2018

Here is how the civility in practice model works:

- Organizations define civility for their context and adopt it as a core value. As such, the organization also defines what respect means, and related values such as humanity, equity, equality, and positive people treatment requirements into its policies and best practices.

- All employees (at all levels) are provided with clear expectations for how to interact with each other, e.g., via codes of conduct, communication plans, aspects of social requirements detailed in job descriptions, etc.
- CRITICAL—employees are not just told how to behave, they are shown, e.g., you cannot simply say, "be polite," "show respect," "don't be racist," "change your tone"—part of the onboarding process must include definitions and modeling of specific aspects of verbal and nonverbal communication skills such that everyone understands what is and is not acceptable.
- Leaders in the organization are the first to be trained so that they can coach their teams appropriately and so that they can lead by example. Civility does not work if leadership is not civil.
- BEFORE "events" such as stress, crisis, illness, safety issues, disengagement, equipment breakdown, and labor shortages happen, that is, when things are going well, leadership is in the habit of building trust, being transparent, teaching civility skills on an ongoing basis, and generally engaging in positive people treatment. This is something that becomes part of the character of the culture, part of every employee's daily experience.
- DURING "events" (examples listed in BEFORE above), leaders do not have to change who they are, how they communicate, their directive approach, or any aspect of how they interact. They continue behaving in a civil manner as they have previously. Their persona and way of interacting has become a standard and is expected. However, if, during a high-risk event, e.g., an emergency or safety issue, a supervisor or manager behaves in an "off-standard" way, there is sufficient trust and collaboration built that his or her team performs as usual and/or jumps in to support, because they recognize that the off-standard behavior is situational. Leaders also work to talk their team through changes and events, coach as they go, be as transparent as possible, and generally work to maintain a high standard of people treatment. This would include learning how to give effective feedback (i.e., the Masotti feedback method).
- AFTER "events," leaders again continue with a civil mindset and behavior and continue to treat people well. Where accolades and acknowledgment are called for, these are given freely, and where

skills gaps were identified, e.g., employees were unable to manage the "event" appropriately, or where mistakes were made, leaders see this as a learning opportunity. They reassess, make a new plan, implement, measure, and repeat.

When civility is applied on an ongoing basis, there are indicators of continuous improvement. Some of the metrics you could watch for as evidence are listed below. Many of these metrics would fall under evaluation categories of return on investment (ROI) and/or return on character (ROC) in the civility in practice model.

INDICATORS OF CONTINUOUS IMPROVEMENT—related to workplace culture and civility.

	Number of incidences before civility practice	Number of incidences after civility practice
• How often do employees feel comfortable asking questions?		
• How often do employees resist directives?		
• How often do supervisors have to repeat directives?		
• How often do supervisors have to engage third-party support to get buy-in from the team (e.g., enlist a team lead to persuade the group)?		
• How often do employees murmur under their breath as the supervisor walks away after giving a directive?		
• How often do employees simply ignore the supervisor?		
• How often do employees nod or gesture agreement but not engage verbally?		
• How often do employees bring or offer the supervisor food or beverage?		
• How often are rude images or words of profanity seen written or drawn around the workplace?		
• How often do employees engage in shop talk in the presence of the supervisor?		
• How often do employees swear?		

Figure 8 Indications of Continuous Improvement (Relative to Civility)©, Masotti, 2019 (Continued)

	Number of incidences before civility practice	Number of incidences after civility practice
• How often do employees ask for feedback, e.g., when it isn't scheduled?		
• How often do employees respond to feedback positively?		
• How often is a default statement used, e.g., during a difficult conversation, "Let me talk to my union rep"?		
• How often do employees defend the supervisor to other employees?		
• How often do employees ask for training in skills required to do their own job?		
• How often do employees ask for training in skills unrelated to their immediate job?		
• How often do employees offer suggestions for improvements?		
• How often do employees call in sick?		
• How often do employees avoid another employee?		
• How often do employees avoid a supervisor?		
• How often do employees exchange physical greetings, e.g., handshake, pat on back, high-five etc.?		
• How often do employees make direct eye contact with supervisors?		
• How often do employees complete required paperwork, and do so in a timely and correct way?		
• How often will employees offer up that they don't know something?		
• How often do employees refer to their supervisor by an unfavorable nickname?		
• How often do employees volunteer useful information before they are asked?		
• How often do employees "push," e.g., be aggressive?		
• How often do employees take a few minutes longer at breaks?		
• How often do employees work slowly to make a point?		
• How often do employees complain about a guideline or rule?		
• How often do employees break a rule, e.g., smoke in the plant?		

Figure 8 Continued

In the Advanced Thinking section at the end of Chapter 3, I shared that in my experience, many of the problems that teams are tasked with solving, the projects that they spend time and money on, would not even have arisen as problems if civility had been embedded into the organizations policies and practices. Examples of this are "low-hanging fruit" problems that often take up many of the resources allocated to continuous improvement, and sadly do not always show good return on investment or long-term benefits.

QUESTION: Based on what you now understand to be incivility, what types of "events" (perceived issues, challenges, crisis, problems) that might be assigned as continuous improvement projects—what we can call "low-hanging fruit"—could be resolved easily through civility, e.g., never get to the point where they are identified as "events"?

QUESTION: Why do you think some supervisors and/or employees would opt NOT to engage in civility best practices in spite of knowing the benefits?

QUESTION: We know from the research that civility at work can increase innovation, retention, trust, and collaboration. What other, more personal or individual, impacts can you perceive if civility becomes part of the employees' day-to-day experience?

QUESTION: What is the risk if civility best practices are not exhibited continuously, that is, before, during, and after an "event"?

See Chapter 9 for Optional Assignment.

Words to Know

- Trident approach
- Incivility
- Social intelligence
- Cultural competence
- Systems thinking
- Continuous learning
- Continuous improvement
- Continual improvement
- Social capital
- Engagement
- Culture indicator continuum

For Review

The Culture Indicator Continuum is an assessment tool devised by Masotti & Bayer in 2019. The tool enables organizations to understand how common behaviors observed on the manufacturing floor (and/or in other workplaces), correlate with overall measures of civility.

Based on previous work completed by the Civility Experts Inc. team (and validated by research conducted by Watson & Wyatt[14]), it has been established that incivility has direct and measurable impacts on retention, safety, productivity, morale, and the bottom line.

Building on this research, via independent field work over 20+ years, Civility Experts Inc. has identified that when trust is low, engagement is low. **Engagement**, according to Civility Experts Inc. refers to intentional, conscious "buying-in" on the part of employees such that because they trust the organization, they choose to come to work, to contribute in a meaningful way, to do more than they are required to, to support their coworkers, and to believe in what the organization stands for and is trying to achieve, even when things are difficult. According to Lew Bayer, CEO of Civility Experts Inc., low trust is often a result of incivility, and the research also shows that when trust or engagement is low, people will be less accountable. For over 20+ years in the field, the team at Civility Experts Inc. has identified specific behaviors and listed these on a civility continuum. These move from positive to negative and reflect the level of engagement.

Generally, the more civil a workplace is, the more positive (+) behaviors are observed.

A few general notes on the engagement continuum:

• **Contribution** means meaningful involvement in achieving specific goals.

---

[14] W. Shadwick, and P. Tate. 2018. "Civility in America 2018: Civility at Work and in Our Public Squares." www.webershandwick.com/wp-content/uploads/2018/06/Civility-in-America-VII-FINAL.pdf.

The Culture Indicator Continuum

BY MASOTTI & BAYER

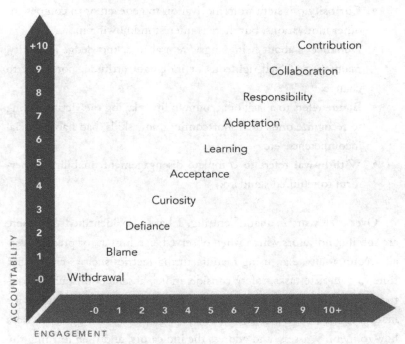

Figure 9 *Civility Indicators Continuum©, Masotti & Bayer 2018*

- **Collaboration** means recognizing one's own and others' skills and talents and opting to contribute (sometimes contributions are not equal).
- **Responsibility** means taking control of one's own choices and managing the consequences of the same.
- **Adaptation** refers to the ability to change, e.g., readiness, hardiness, resilience, and self-management basics.
- **Learning** means self-directing, and/or adopting opportunities to learn and grow—this stage requires a recognition that one is deficit in a skill area and there is a recognition of the value of addressing that gap.
- **Acceptance** is a neutral stage where one identifies what he or she can control and recognizes that he or she can choose to go forward or go backward.

NOTE: Learning and acceptance phases represent a "thinking hinge" or a mindset shift.

- **Curiosity** can stem from motivation to get even or to compete or other motivations, but there is interest in knowing more.
- **Defiance** is about being angry, refusal to acknowledge authority, maintaining a self-righteous or indignant attitude, not ready to change.
- **Blame** refers to a lack of accountability, playing the victim, failing to recognize one's own shortcomings, low skills, bad habits, social incompetence, etc.
- **Withdrawal** refers to complete disengagement, inability to perform to required standard.

Over 20+ years in manufacturing, I have also identified that there are specific indicators which when observed, can hint at, or predict overall accountability, e.g., using manufacturing metrics such as error rates, time to complete tasks, safety considerations, absenteeism, quality controls, overall productivity, etc. Generally, supervisors are accountable for managing the people side of manufacturing and so teaching supervisors how to identify, assess, and address the indicators, and then learning the root cause of those indicators can help manage performance, and change workplace culture.

IMPORTANT TO KNOW: Combining the aspects of trust/engagement and accountability results in a predictive continuum.

How Do You Use the Continuum?

For each of the 10 states on the continuum, there are typical behavioral indicators including verbal and nonverbal gestures. The best approach would be to first assess supervisors and managers to see where they sit on the continuum. Clearly, leadership should strive to, and be required to, score high in the upper right quadrant, that is, on collaboration and contribution.

Next, supervisors and managers would OBSERVE employees on the job and watch for indicators.

State/ behavior	Indicators	Possible causes for state/ behavior in individual	Possible contributing conditions, e.g., behavior of leader or context	Skills to teach to offset (low end of continuum) or reinforce (high end of continuum)
Withdrawal	Avoiding eye contact Don't say hello Sabotage Calling in sick Disengaging from optional and/or social activities at work Backing away Being silent Avoiding saying "I don't know" Not performing Increased errors	Low confidence Social anxiety Illness Depression Passive aggression Embarrassment	"Human" needs not met, e.g., Maslow's hierarchy Ignoring Unnecessary punishment Leading by fear Cultural nuances Shaming or embarrassing Personal bias	Safety Fair wages Communication Self-management basics Systems-thinking, e.g., related to consequences/impact to team Assessments, e.g., related to competence Teach SOPs
Blame	Calling someone names Pointing fingers (literal) Accusing Deflecting Making excuses Criticizing Yelling Murmuring under breath Filing complaints Feigning injuries Giving part of information Withholding details	Low competence Anger Disappointment Misunderstanding of conditions/situation Poor team relationships Lack of clarity about responsibilities	Focus on fault-finding versus looking for resolutions Favoritism Lack of clarity in delegation Setting people up to fail	Systems thinking Responsibility Asking questions Relational impact, e.g., of shirking responsibility Building trust Clarify roles and expectations Encourage clarifying questions Hold people accountable, e.g., consequences

(continued)

***Figure 10** Civility Continuum Chart©, Masotti & Bayer 2018*

Figure 10 Continued

State/behavior	Indicators	Possible causes for state/behavior in individual	Possible contributing conditions, e.g., behavior of leader or context	Skills to teach to offset (low end of continuum) or reinforce (high end of continuum)
	Poor quality output Increased errors Taking too long to complete tasks Focusing on problems Red face Strong gestures Wide stance			
Defiance	Sighing Gesturing widely Harrumphing stomping foot Walking away Turning one's back Averting eyes Hiding tools Not showing up for work Speaking negatively Breaking rules Not following processes Working slower or not at all Swearing Not wearing required safety items Giving short, incomplete answers Word splice, e.g., looking for a reason not to be direct or truthful Glaring Clenched fists or jaw Physical aggression	Low respect for authority Ego, e.g., getting even Anger Disappointment Peer pressure	Low trust Poor rapport Ego-orientation Unfair treatment Failure to explain reasons for things fully Aggression or assertive demeanor Body language or posture is overpowering Bullying behavior Failing to apologize	Systems thinking Social IQ Emotional IQ Anger management Communication skills, e.g., crucial conversations Define respectful behavior related to defiance

Curiosity	Asking questions Smiling Actively listening Observing others Snooping Reaching out to new people he or she usually doesn't talk to Asking for more work Coming early Staying late Interest in solution Increased patience/stamina/persistence	Genuine interest Need to improve	Approachable style Makes information available Encourages questions Answers truthfully Transparency Learns about team	Finding information Continuous learning strategies Asking questions Listening skills Self-directed learning strategies Social radar Open responses to facts Provide learning opportunities
Acceptance	Being silent Nodding Smiling Stating agreement or acceptance Interacting positively with others Speaking positively about issue/people Showing appreciation Recognizing others, e.g., when good things happen Improvements in health Seems less stressed	Contentment Satisfaction with job assignment Respect for position Respect for authority	Trust Accurate skills assessment History of honesty Shows genuine care for employees, e.g., psychological and physical safety Be positive Focus on benefit but be truthful about risks and impact	Mentorship, e.g., how to teach others Treat as adults Show appreciation for trust Action-oriented
Learning	Asking questions Studying/reading Collecting information Attending training	Understanding that change is inevitable Wanting to succeed Vying for new position	Coaches Provides opportunities to learn Adapts to communication and learning styles	Continuous learning strategies Coaching skills Provide opportunities to learn

(continued)

Figure 10 Continued

State/ behavior	Indicators	Possible causes for state/ behavior in individual	Possible contributing conditions, e.g., behavior of leader or context	Skills to teach to offset (low end of continuum) or reinforce (high end of continuum)
	Observing others Practicing Trying new things Offering solutions Sharing information and learning	Genuine interest	Offers full explanations Allows others to learn from mistakes Celebrates achievement Cross-trains Good communication skills	
Adaptation	Asking questions Managing stress, e.g., stays calm Seeking to understand, e.g., listens and asks questions Showing resilience Expressing positive attitude about change Learning from others Seems calm	Trusts leaders Believes in organizational goals Supports team Willing to learn and bend to keep job	Provides full information when possible Teaches stress management Encourages hardiness and resilience (and exhibits it) Builds trust Addresses Maslow's needs Monitors tone on radio and in person; shows restraint	Reward and/or incentive Create safe place, e.g., psychological Manage change fatigue Be transparent
Responsibility	Accepting one's role and contribution Exercising personal power, e.g., decision-making Contributing to the work and goals Smiles Eye contact Expresses pride in work Maintains high standards Adheres to policy Recognizes authority Doesn't question assignments Seeks to improve	Maturity Holding on to tenure Recognizes value of staying employees Wants respect of peers Personal values	Treats people like adults Sets and adheres to standards Is consistent Shows respect Leads by example Gives options Uses adult learning principles Manages privacy Sets clear expectations Rewards honesty and fair play Encourages mastery Allows for pride of work	Verbal praise Fair wages Personal privileges were acceptable Promotions

Collaboration	Identifying one's own skills and expertise Acknowledging skills and expertise of others Seeking to understand Willing to share credit Physical and verbal "pats" on the back Increased socialization	Feels valued Recognizes each individual can make a difference Has identified personal contributions Sees long-term benefits of working together	Identifies individual skills Acknowledges individual contributions Shares goals Creates space for interaction Fosters positive communication Recognizes the value of debate Doesn't micro-manage Thanks for contribution	Benefits of respect Civil discourse Debating skills Social radar skills
Contribution	Seeing the value of the work Acknowledging the work of others Accepting awards and recognition Expresses pride in work Speaks highly of the organization in the community Takes on social roles (unpaid) Refers others to the organization Regular attendance Covers for others Stays at job even when there is no outside incentive	High engagement Values work team Respects leadership Respect for self Understands whole is greater than sum of the parts	Celebrates success Gives credit where credit is due Encourages initiatives Creates positive environment where people will engage Thanks people Lets people be autonomous when possible	Give reward Offer acknowledgment Mentorship

To move individual employees through the continuum, supervisors and leaders must be able to:

- Set clear expectations for accountability, e.g., what behaviors are expected?
- Observe the employee on the job, e.g., set aside time specifically to watch people work.
- Identify "off-standard" behavior, e.g., note symptoms indicating the extent to which an employee is, or is not, falling into a category on the continuum.
- Assess the cause of the behavior—is it a skills gap, an attitude issue, or some other factor, e.g., related to situation, equipment, or circumstance?
- Give feedback (positive or negative), e.g., to redirect behavior where necessary.

In addition, the organization overall must support and require that leaders have a "learning mindset." Specifically, supervisors/managers must adopt an attitude whereby they:

- Assume they can (and will) learn something, e.g., from someone else
- Are willing to admit when they don't know something
- Don't make assumptions about why people may or may not immediately help/support them, e.g., it may have nothing to do with the leader
- Remember how important it is to earn trust
- Agree that respect is something everyone deserves, e.g., it does not have to be earned
- Acknowledge the intellect and experience of others
- Ask how they can help the other person, e.g., "help him help you" (this is sometimes a test of one's integrity)
- Speak in facts and information and avoid opinion
- Thank people for trusting them and doing the right thing (but don't say, "Hey, you did the right thing," which could come off as assumptive or condescending or parental, depending on the tone)
- Credit (in their presence and/or to others) those who support and help them

Once this civil attitude has been established and when it is exhibited consistently, leaders build trust with their teams such that they are more successful in their communications and coaching and they are able to move employees along the continuum.

How to Use the Continuum as a Continuous Learning Tool

1. The workplace can assess each supervisor's team, e.g., identify where on the grid the individuals sit and identify a pattern.
2. Based on the pattern, e.g., a cluster around a negative state, supervisors can be made aware of:
   a. Behaviors or conditions that they are contributing to that are resulting in the indicators
   b. Behaviors to watch out for in individual employees
3. Leaders can be trained in what to watch out for, what it means, and how to address it.
4. Employees can be trained in specific skill areas that will enable them to move through the stages.

A key message for supervisors and managers is that if your teams are not performing well, this is a direct reflection on you. A supervisor MUST be held accountable for these issues. Specifically, aspects of expectation for people management should be written right into supervisors' performance evaluations.

As one example, if a manager tells a supervisor, "We need you to be more engaged," or "We need you to get your team more engaged," what does that mean? Supervisors need to understand what engagement is and what the indicators of engagement are. If their teams are not engaged, they need to figure out how they (the supervisor) are contributing to, or causing the disengagement, and/or they need to figure out what contextual or situational factors are contributing to it. And then they need to address this. From firsthand experience on the job, Christian Masotti says, "I can state with certainty, that the more engaged people are, the more accountable they are, and the more likely they are to meet their key performance indicators (KPIs)."

Supervisors should do an analysis of each person on his or her team and find out where they are on the continuum. The next step is to correlate and implement some corrective action. Improvements would be indicated by movement on the continuum, so supervisors should assess, track, and analyze the data on an ongoing basis—as often as every month—and work to improve the overall levels of civility continuously.

How Much Do You Remember?

1. Companies that openly promote civil communication among employees earn how much more revenue than competitors?
   a. 22 percent
   b. 87 percent
   c. 55 percent
   d. 30 percent
2. When embedded into workplace training, policy, procedures, and best practices, civility is:
   a. retroactive
   b. reactive
   c. protractive
   d. proactive
3. In the civility in practice model, "ROI" refers to:
   a. regularly observed incident
   b. return on currency
   c. recommended occupation indicator
   d. return on character
4. Calling someone names, accusing, and deflecting are behaviors that suggest an employee is at what state on the culture indicator continuum?
   a. Withdrawal
   b. Adaptation
   c. Blame
   d. Defiance

Recommended Reading

Ahlstrom, J. 2014. *How to Succeed with Continuous Improvement*. New York, NY: McGraw-Hill Education.

Homework Assignment

Continuous improvement, sometimes called continual improvement, is the ongoing improvement of products, services, or processes through incremental and breakthrough improvements.

There are many tools used for continuous improvement, but one popular four-step model is called the Deming Cycle.

Write a 2,000-word essay on tools for continuous improvement and include notes on the history of, and differences between:

- The Deming Cycle
- Six Sigma
- Lean
- Total Quality Management

Advanced Thinking—Preparing for Chapter 5

In real life at work, I have learned that most people just want to feel valued, trusted, and respected. If you can achieve this and be perceived as a decent human being, most other attributes account for very little. The fact is, supervisors and leaders would have a much easier job if they acknowledged and leveraged the skills and experience of their teams. When supervisors spend all their time working to please one or two higher-ups at the expense of building trust and collaboration with the significantly larger group they support, they are neglecting their biggest assets.

Why do you think so many leaders/managers/supervisors do not properly leverage the skills and knowledge of their teams?

CHAPTER 5

Embedding Civil Communication

Don't discount the power of your words. The thought that they might cause unnecessary hurt or discomfort should inform every conversation.

—P.M. Forni.

Ultimately, incorporating a companywide change initiative to build a **culture of civility** includes:

- Reworking organizational policy that may in fact be encouraging and fostering incivility and inhumane practices
- Eliminating time spent on disciplinary and corrective paperwork
- Fostering a culture of learning versus a culture of fear
- Building attitudes that support skills for eliminating defects and rework (MUDA)
- Utilizing communication strategies that result in collaboration, civility, and clarity
- Instilling practices for documentation that are concise, accurate, and civil
- Reducing tension between leadership/management and employees by creating new civility-focused patterns for communication

But changing all of these internal structures will take time and so while these changes are underway, organizations can begin to teach their leadership team civil communication skills.

To facilitate positive interactions, individuals at all levels of the organization, (but ideally starting at the top) would have to be encouraged to take on civility as a core value. This is achieved through civility training. (You may recall civility training as prong/step #1 in the Trident Approach).

Once the leadership team has endorsed civility, which would include accepting that civility training is required, each individual would need to be assessed in four core civility skill areas: cultural competence, social intelligence, systems thinking, and continuous learning. And then, where skills gaps are identified, the organization would provide strategic, specific, and customized civility training to address those gaps.

Once individuals are fully engaged by way of adopting a civility mindset and acknowledging the value of, and accountability for, civility, they start to behave in ways that change their own experience but also the experience of those around them, and the workplace culture begins to shift.

Some of the civil behaviors that are exhibited include:

- Being honest
- Treating others equally
- Being empathetic
- Self-directing their own learning
- Listening with TING
- ....and so on (please see the civility value chain chart- Figure 11)

And even without formal training, leaders can be encouraged to take some immediate actions that can start to shift the culture. These actions may include:

- Showing consideration for each other, e.g., other supervisors and their higher-ups. Just start with basic greetings and acknowledgment.
- Showing consideration for the workplace teams, e.g., not just their own teams. Say hello, smile, make eye contact.
- Learning to apologize, sincerely.
- Waiting for employees to respond—that is, listen—when you ask a question or for suggestions, etc.
- Acknowledging the suggestions of the team and giving updates about what is being done with the suggestions. If people don't see

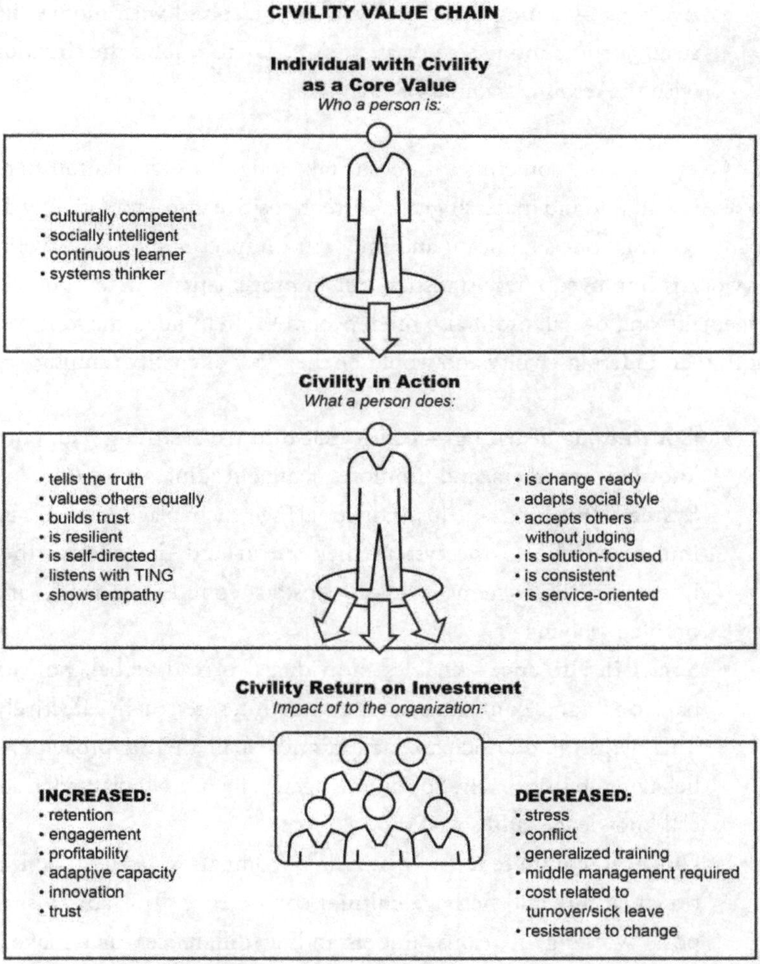

CIVILITY VALUE CHAIN

**Individual with Civility
as a Core Value**
Who a person is:

- culturally competent
- socially intelligent
- continuous learner
- systems thinker

Civility in Action
What a person does:

- tells the truth
- values others equally
- builds trust
- is resilient
- is self-directed
- listens with TING
- shows empathy

- is change ready
- adapts social style
- accepts others
  without judging
- is solution-focused
- is consistent
- is service-oriented

Civility Return on Investment
Impact of to the organization:

INCREASED:
- retention
- engagement
- profitability
- adaptive capacity
- innovation
- trust

DECREASED:
- stress
- conflict
- generalized training
- middle management required
- cost related to
  turnover/sick leave
- resistance to change

Figure 11 Civility Value Chain©, Masotti & Bayer 2018

any movement or action, they eventually just give up offering help and/or suggestions.

- Providing easy access to information that employees need to do their jobs; don't withhold details or information that could expedite understanding or activity.
- Avoiding immediately dismissing opinions. You don't always have to agree or respond, but if people don't feel heard, they will bypass the chain of command and share their opinions with the team or go to the union.

- Avoiding assuming every problem can be solved with money; instead, assume money is not an option. Try to resolve the situation with the resources you have.

Over time, and sometimes it doesn't take long, the organization starts to see measurable and increasingly consistent positive impacts of civility. In manufacturing, one significant and important impact of increased civility at work is improved safety statistics, but improvements in retention, engagement, and overall profit also often occur. As a reminder, the four core skills that underpin civility and would be the focus of civility training are:

- **Continuous learning**—fosters self-directed learning, supports knowledge workers, and promotes change readiness.
- **Systems thinking**—helps individuals see their place, power, and impact relative to the system they are in and the systems they interact with. Systems thinking fosters confidence, trust, and problem-solving.
- **Social intelligence**—enables individuals to read verbal, nonverbal, tonal, and contextual cues and to interpret them effectively. This helps them anticipate, adapt, and repair their approach and behavior appropriately. Social intelligence includes social radar, social knowledge, and social style.
- **Cultural competence**—This skill encompasses both organizational culture and heritage cultural competence. This ability supports working in teams, understanding differences that make a difference, recognizing where process overrides preference, and generally helps promote respect at work.

The recommendation for manufacturing organizations where command and control management style might be deeply ingrained, is to focus on social intelligence training. In a very short time, this strategic training can build skills such that there is immediate measurable impact on the workplace culture—specifically on the overall **"tone"** of communications.

Communication is an essential skill for leaders at any level in manufacturing. But for supervisors who are responsible for managing the production team this skill becomes critical. And yet, many manufacturing organizations do not spend sufficient time and resources ensuring that their leaders are effective communicators.

LMA Consulting Group, Claremont, California, has released the *Manufacturing and Distribution Skills Gap Report*, based on a skills gap survey conducted in conjunction with the APICS Inland Empire chapter that focused on how manufacturers and distributors are adjusting to the new "business normal" in terms of their workforces.

The survey, which asked hiring managers and human resources professionals about recruiting, training, and general employment trends in manufacturing and distribution, revealed that many of the soft skills needed to be a successful manufacturing employee were lacking in both existing workers and potential new hires. For current employers, 77.7 percent of respondents stated that their own employees lack basic presentation and communications skills needed to be successful in their current positions and that this lack of skill would impact future professional movement within the organization.

Closely following a gap in communication skills is the inability to problem-solve or come up with ideas or alternatives to a situation or issue. In general, the manufacturing workforce is asking for direction from supervisors or managers rather than initiating new ideas and solutions.

Core communication skill requirements of employers have not changed much over time. But the emphasis on collaborative work has altered dramatically. A Harvard Business Review study found that the time managers and employees spend on collaborative activities has increased by more than 50 percent in the past 20 years.

A closer and more comprehensive review of skills gaps across organizational groups—initially undertaken as a means of understanding why these workplaces were uncivil—has informed the Civility Experts Inc. team that when general communication, problem-solving, and collaboration skills are lacking, one way to improve and encourage interactions at work is to make training in social intelligence a priority. This is because social intelligence teaches people the following skills which can offset communication skills gaps, enables people who can't problem solve on their own to ask questions, and builds trust such that people can collaborate more effectively.

Social intelligence training enables people to:

- Read verbal, nonverbal, contextual, and situational cues to interpret the moods, motivations, and needs of others
- Exhibit nonverbal, verbal, and situational cues appropriately
- Be present and pay attention to what is going on around them
- Recognize when gestures, language, behavior, or approach is grounded in culture, generation, or gender nuances
- Pick up on very subtle changes in tone and behavior to sense when a mood shifts
- Learn unwritten rules—unspoken and unwritten expectations for how to live in a certain environment, e.g., aspects of workplace culture
- Learn written and known rules, e.g., codes of conduct, regulation etc.
- Become self-aware of one's own social style
- Adapt one's social style to what is appropriate or required for a certain situation
- Adapt to change quickly due to ability to shift social gears when necessary
- Respond to events calmly due to ability to anticipate and/or monitor
- Recognize appropriate time to ask questions
- See aspects of personality that are otherwise unnoticed
- Send positive first impression
- Make others feel at ease
- Build trust, e.g., by paying attention
- Be a better listener
- Be cordial and approachable
- Show humility, and recognize when help is needed
- Read emotions, and be empathetic when needed

When leaders in manufacturing have high social intelligence combined with some experience interacting with others in the workplace context—for example, they know the general expectations for the workplace culture, they know the industry jargon, have some knowledge of the terms and processes, etc.,—they can apply their social intelligence in a way that fosters **social acuity**.

Indicators of Social Acuity

Leaders need to have high "social acuity," that is, they need to have a keen social sense. They must be consistently accurate and timely in their perceptions and assessments of social settings. They need to know how to:

- Read contextual cues
- Be attentive to the nuances of workplace culture
- Navigate politics in union environments
- Identify who will be an ally and who will be a challenge
- Build trust
- Repair when a trust is broken
- Consider contextual aspects when timing everything from greetings, to feedback to workplace coaching and performance reviews
- Communicate in a way that leaves everyone involved in the interaction feeling valued
- Acknowledge differences that make a difference, e.g., related to gender, culture, generation
- Give timely and effective feedback
- Monitor and manage nonverbal cues to boost credibility and perceived competence
- Adapt a supervisory approach and style to meet the needs of individual workers
- Apply adult learning principles
- Maintain credibility as a leader but still be perceived as approachable by the production team

One of the outcomes of high social acuity is a recognition that each individual in an organization has value. But we have to be careful not to attach only monetary value to individuals. In *Doing Virtuous Business*, Theodore Roosevelt Malloch states that,

Every person has a fingerprint of personality and potential and desire to contribute. When we define people solely in economic terms, our motivational and incentive schemes tend to become mechanical and manipulative. We try to define a system that will idiot-proof the process, which can in turn make people feel like idiots.

And *Fortune Magazine* recently described the soulless company as suffering from an enemy within.

From a civility perspective, each individual of course has value as a human being. As such, every individual is deserving of respect just because he or she is human and on the planet. (Trust, however, is something that must be earned and not every person is deserving of trust). In terms of workplace value, individuals at all levels should be acknowledged for:

- Potential (amount of potential might vary)
- Intelligence (nature of intelligence might vary)
- Education (type and extent of education might vary)
- Social contribution (nature and volume of social contribution might vary)
- Experience (time on the job and type of experience might vary)
- Resilience (extent of resilience might vary)

All of these elements are aspects of value BUT it is each individual's understanding of civility, and his or her choosing to be civil that enables us to recognize and appreciate these aspects of value. Without civility, and without respect, people often fail to see the value of others. As such, it is important to also recognize what Civility Experts Inc. CEO Lew Bayer describes as **Civility quotient**.

Civility commitment + civility competency (both might vary) = Civility quotient

The idea is that when everyone in a workplace understands that each individual has value

For Consideration: The Civility Value Chain

In real life at work, I have learned that most people just want to feel valued, trusted, and respected. If you can achieve this and be perceived as a decent human being, most other attributes account for very little. The fact is, supervisors and leaders would have a much easier job if they acknowledged and leveraged the skills and experience of their teams. Each individual has the potential and often the opportunity to impact the culture around him or her. This is because every interaction, every conversation, even every conflict, becomes part of an individual's experience. When interactions are more positive than negative, we see significant and long-lasting shifts in overall workplace culture.

When supervisors spend all their time working to please one or two higher-ups at the expense of building trust and collaboration with the significantly larger group they support, they are neglecting their biggest assets.

QUESTION: Why do many leaders/managers/supervisors not properly leverage the skills and knowledge of their teams?

QUESTION: What can happen if leaders do not agree that every person is equally deserving of respect?

QUESTION: What happens if an individual is lacking in one of the four skills required to be civility-competent?

See Chapter 9 for Optional Assignment.

Words to Know

- Incivility
- Culture of civility
- Tone
- Social intelligence
- Social acuity
- Civility quotient
- Civility value chain

For Review

Clearly it takes time to build communication skills and when contexts and teams are continually changing, a person must apply continuous learning in order to keep up with expectations and to be effective in various settings. Building on 20+ years in manufacturing, Christian Masotti has compiled a social competence toolkit for manufacturing supervisors that includes 10 communication strategies with ready-to-use checklists. Review and application of these tools can expedite a supervisor's ability to acquire critical communication skills. Take some time to review the charts and assess yourself on your overall civil communication skills.

Masotti Commonsense Social Competence Strategy #1: Wait for It

This strategy is about pausing—being deliberate about being present, listening, and suspending judgment.

- Pause deliberately to assess the situation.
- Resist saying anything immediately.
- Suspend your thoughts, e.g., don't make assumptions, don't jump to conclusions, set aside any biases or expectations.
- Listen to the other person.
- Pay attention to the context, e.g., what is going on around you?
- Watch the other person's nonverbal cues.
- Ask questions using a calm, polite tone.
- Avoid starting your sentences with "I" in an effort to be other-focused.
- Be self-aware. Pay attention to when you make snap judgments and work to understand why you have jumped to conclusions and then set those judgments aside.

Masotti Commonsense Social Competence Strategy #2: Just Be Nice

This strategy is about extending common courtesies and choosing to be "human-kind."

- Pause, wait…take a breath, compose yourself, think about what you will say or do BEFORE you do it.
- Assume the best of others; try to set aside any personal issues, history with the individual, personal needs, known biases, etc.
- Consider social protocol. What do the social rules (written or unwritten) suggest is the appropriate response or behavior in this setting and/or situation?

- Think about what you want to happen next, e.g., how do you want to be perceived, how do you want the other person to feel, what do you want the outcome of the interaction/communication to be?
- Consider the time and place, e.g., is this the right time for the communication? Should you go somewhere private? Do you need a third party to witness? Does the other party need time to compose him or herself?
- Be kind.
  ○ Choose words and/or actions that show you at your best and do not cause harm to the other person.
  ○ Make eye contact as a way of acknowledging others.
  ○ Extend general greetings, e.g., say hello.
  ○ Maintain a calm and moderate tone, e.g., don't yell.
  ○ Avoid swearing.
- Close with a verbal or physical handshake, e.g., shake hands, say thank you for X, look the person in the eye, OR, acknowledge and close the interaction verbally; e.g., say, "So, we are all good then?" or "See you tomorrow then," or something to show you anticipate a positive and future interaction.

Masotti Commonsense Social Competence Strategy #3: Get Out There and Talk to People

This strategy is about being intentional in how you engage with others socially.

- Always keep your head up when passing others or walking through a workspace, halls, parking lot, etc.
- Even if you don't know people, make it your habit to glance at them. Practice noticing things about people; what they're wearing, their expressions, etc.
- Practice keeping an approachable, friendly look on your face.
- Be deliberate about exhibiting open postures—don't sit with your arms crossed, take your hands out of your pockets, remove sunglasses when talking to people indoors, extend an open palm for a handshake.
- When you know people (even if you don't know their names) make eye contact and smile.

- If you can't stop to talk, wave or nod hello, but don't ask a question such as, "How are you?" while you continue walking or moving.
- If you have time, stop and chat. Stop. Turn your shoulders square with the other person, greet him or her, move to within 24 inches of the other person, and engage. Set aside all other distractions while you do so.
- If you have to break eye contact or move your attention to someone or something else for a minute, e.g., check your watch, or acknowledge another person, say, "excuse me" before you do it, or say, "sorry about that" after you do it.
- As you are chatting, make it a point to focus on the other person. Ask him or her questions and wait for the answers. Try to avoid talking about yourself.
- If you didn't shake hands when you greeted the person, and when context and culture suggest it's appropriate, extend an exit handshake.
- If you are legitimately busy, don't stop and pretend to pay attention. Simply state that you are glad to see the person, but are unable to visit at this time, and then wish the person a happy day and move on.

Masotti Commonsense Social Competence Strategy #4: Apply Continuous Learning to Connect with People

This strategy is about recognizing that every interaction is a learning opportunity.

- Treat people with respect from the beginning so that when you need to approach them for help, they see you as someone they can trust who values them.
- Assume that someone, at some time, somewhere has experienced this same situation.
- Assume that you are not the only person to have an idea.
- Always ask the people doing the job, ask them directly, face-to-face.
- Approach people at the appropriate time.
- Be respectful in your tone; don't assume people have an obligation to help you just because you are a supervisor.

- Ask targeted questions, e.g., not open-ended ones.
- Admit you need help.
- Listen for answers—don't interrupt, don't criticize or apply your personal biases, opinions, or beliefs.
- Don't dismiss anyone; you never know what information will be useful down the road. Even if the information being shared at the time is not relevant, use the interaction as an opportunity to build rapport and trust.
- Consider that one person may not have all the answers, but the collective probably does.
- Acknowledge the sharing and the information, and let the person sharing with you know you appreciate their help.
- Give credit when you use the information down the road.
- Share the information with others, e.g., don't hoard it now that you have it.
- Avoid going back to the same person more than once, as this can cause strain within the team. Instead build a relationship with each member of the team; this builds credibility.

Masotti Commonsense Social Competence Strategy #5: Always Tell the Truth

This strategy is about relational wealth. If you want to build trust, here are some communication habits you should adopt:

- Make a point to be honest with everyone, not just some people.
- Be consistent, e.g., always tell the truth—don't pick and choose when to be honest.
- Be honest when delivering both good and bad news.
- Be direct, tell the whole truth versus a piece or version of the truth, e.g., instead of saying you are being fired for lateness, an indirect version is saying, "You know, lateness is one of the metrics we watch."
- Assume the best of people, but don't immediately trust everything people say; ask strategic questions.
- Look people in the eye when you are communicating the truth.
- Be deliberate in your communication—choose your words carefully and say exactly what you mean; don't sugarcoat or be vague.

- Avoid pretending you have authority or power you don't have; be honest about your abilities and influence.
- Do your due diligence before making promises—ensure you can follow through before you say what you can and will do.
- Pick an appropriate time to be truthful.
- Consider privacy and confidentiality.
- Monitor your tone, e.g., don't be harsh.
- Avoid apologizing for telling the truth, e.g., "I'm sorry to have to tell you X, but…"
- Give people a minute to absorb what you are telling them.
- Keep being truthful even when others are dishonest, and/or even when no one seems to notice. People do notice, and there is often documentation to support your efforts.

Masotti Commonsense Social Competence Strategy #6: Ask Strategic Questions

This strategy is about acknowledging that you can't know everything; you must be able to ask for help.

- See people as resources. Assume you can learn from them.
- Be clear in your own mind about what exactly you need to know—what information are you seeking?
- Watch for the appropriate time to approach someone to ask questions, e.g., don't bother employees right before lunch or during lunch or breaks. This is their personal time and they may resent your intrusion. Consider approaching at the end of the shift or just after a break or lunch.
- Consider privacy and confidentiality.
- Do not interrupt when the other person is talking.
- Don't assume you already know the answer to the question you are asking.
- Don't assume that the answer is correct or factual—be sure.
- Don't assume that only one person has the answer or information you seek. Ask more than one person if possible.
- Don't assume that one person speaks for the whole group.

- Monitor your postures and nonverbal communication when listening, e.g., avoid condescending or impatient gestures.
- Listen with TING.
- Ask a specific question and start with one question only. Avoid bombarding the person with many questions at once.
- Choose a specific question for a specific purpose, e.g.,
  ○ Ask a "how is your day" question to gauge morale or attitude.
  ○ Ask a "get to the point" question to hold someone accountable for a misbehavior.
  ○ Ask a "what would happen if" question to get someone to share information or help resolve a problem.
- Don't expect a thank you and don't say things like, "You owe me one"—extend the gesture with no expectation of reciprocity.

Masotti Commonsense Social Competence Strategy #7: Build Resilience (Learn to Take a Punch)

This strategy is about being of strong will, staying positive, and not taking things too personally.

- Show people how the work they do is valued on the job, e.g., why is enduring the hardship worth it?
- Make people aware of the types of challenges they may face on the job.
- Provide opportunities for people to see how others managed those challenges in the past.
- Build your own resilience and model resilient behavior. For example:
  ○ Have a positive attitude.
  ○ Name your fears and face them.
  ○ Set small achievable personal ongoing goals so that you can experience success.
  ○ Encourage others and foster optimism.
  ○ Don't take yourself too seriously; have a sense of humor.
  ○ Take advantage of social supports around you; ask for help when you need it.
- Encourage autonomy.

- Provide opportunities to practice coping strategies.
- Build "time out" opportunities into daily routine; make sure people get breaks.
- Incorporate positive language, such as affirmations, into workplace slogans and mottos.
- Provide team supports, e.g., buddy and mentor programs.

Masotti Commonsense Social Competence Strategy #8: Foster Collaboration

This strategy is about how to build engagement and rapport.

- Be approachable.
- Don't take yourself too seriously.
- Be able to say, "I don't know."
- Be transparent.
- Assume there are people in the room smarter than you are.
- Acknowledge the experience, skills, and credentials of others.
- Be curious and ask questions.
- Ask for help.
- Take notes, show that you are serious about the information you are seeking.
- Review the processes that support collaboration.
- Offer support, with no strings attached.
- Be honest about what you know.
- Share what you know.
- Stick to the facts when you can, avoid opinions.
- Thank others who share with you.
- Credit others with information they share with you that you pass on.
- Strive to exceed expectations, i.e., give more than is required.
- Implement processes to ensure that all collaborators have an opportunity to share.
- Set ground rules for communication in collaboration settings.
- Invite varied opinions and discussion—disagreement is sometimes a good thing.
- Encourage wild ideas, creativity, and innovation.

- Create a psychologically safe environment where others feel free to speak.
- Maintain confidentiality where applicable.

Masotti Commonsense Social Competence Strategy #9: Be Hardy

This strategy is about recognizing your physical and mental limitations and planning for them.

- Anticipate and plan for a physically demanding environment, e.g., consider what you and/or your team need in order to work well, related to:
  - Noise
  - Deadlines
  - Moving equipment
  - Moving vehicles
  - Ventilation: quality and noise associated with it
  - Repetitive motion
  - Safety equipment that hinders movement
  - Physical barriers to communication
  - Tight spaces
  - Large, open spaces
  - Difficulty related to equipment
  - Range of motion required
  - Time standing
  - Distance to areas you need to go to on the job, e.g., parking to work site
  - Availability of washrooms
  - Allowable breaks
  - Allergens
  - Chemicals
  - General morale
  - Temperature in the room
  - Availability of food and water
  - Availability of first aid or emergency equipment
- Take care of your personal needs. For example:
  - Sleep when you can and for a reasonable amount of time.

- Keep up with regular body maintenance—visit the dentist, eye doctor, doctor.
- Have a supply of any required medications on hand.
- Exercise regularly.
- Eat a healthy diet.
- Practice effective stress management.
- Practice good hygiene, e.g., hair, nails, shaving, etc.
- Make it a habit to keep clothes clean and in good repair.
- Maintain safety standards, e.g., wear safety equipment.

- Look out for typical "look and behavior" when you or others are doing the job. If there is variance, or off-standard look and behavior, consider if that behavior is impacting performance. If it is, you need to address what you are seeing.
  - You don't need to know the reason; you just identify and call out the behavior, to prevent an injury, for example.
  - Ask questions to discover the causes of off-standard behavior, e.g., due to:
    - Drugs
    - Alcohol
    - Nervous breakdown
    - High stress
    - External situation, e.g., personal trauma
    - Illness
    - Depression
    - Hunger
    - Exhaustion
    - Distress

Masotti Commonsense Social Competence Strategy #10: Be Responsible

This strategy is about being an adult at work—recognizing you are accountable and approaching your work with maturity.

- Run your own race: Decide what you want out of life and make a plan to achieve it.

- Establish personal standards. For example:
  - Have a morning routine.
  - Exercise daily.
  - Eat healthy.
  - Only take jobs that pay a minimum of X.
  - Do not engage in, or endorse, illegal activities.
  - Pay what I owe.
- Establish personal policies. For example:
  - Do not lie.
  - Always do more than is expected.
  - Always consider how my actions will impact others.
  - Never steal.
  - Always save someone else some hardship or misery if I can.
  - Give without expecting anything in return.
- Clarify expectations of others.
- Make promises, but only if you can keep them.
- Learn to say no.
- Learn to apologize.
- Accept compliments.
- Accept apologies from others.
- Invite feedback.
- Learn from mistakes.
- Forgive yourself for mistakes.
- Accept that you can't fix/help/save everyone; people have to learn to take responsibility for themselves.
- Be sure you know what your specific responsibilities are, e.g., job tasks.
- Take ownership of our own learning.

How Much Do You Remember?

1. Social intelligence includes:
   a. social skills, social smarts, and social savvy
   b. social style, social knowledge, and social savvy
   c. social knowledge, social radar, and social style
   d. social radar, social skills, and social style

2. One behavior that builds trust when communicating is:
   a. Always tell the truth.
   b. Look people in the eye.
   c. Say what you mean.
   d. All of the above.
3. Respect means:
   a. everyone is treated equitably.
   b. everyone is treated as valuable.
   c. everyone is trusted.
   d. everyone is given equal opportunities.
4. In the civility value chain, what a person does (in terms of civility) is called:
   a. action-oriented civility
   b. civility in action
   c. civil action
   d. actionable civility

Recommended Reading

Masott, C., and L. Bayer. 2020. *Manufacturing Civility*. Winnipeg, MB, Canada: Propriety Publishing.

Homework Assignment

Review the following scenario, and then assess the pros and cons of the two different approaches to continuous improvement and describe how the approaches may have impacted overall communication. For example, was the process civil? Did it foster collaboration or was it competitive?

At manufacturing company X you are required to have one continuous improvement project a month with $100,000 savings per year. Everyone's projects and progress is charted on the wall with everyone's faces and details posted for the entire work team to see.

• If you did not complete the project and not save $100,000, there was potential for you to be let go.

- Everyone on the team was in the same situation and had the support of one continuous improvement manager whose job was to support the projects.
- Because everyone was in the same situation, supervisors always discussed and talked about projects and teams. If someone was stuck for ideas, other supervisors would make observations and through discussion would help to identify suitable projects for each other in their own specific zones.
- The process was collaborative and was a great success.

At manufacturing company Y, completion of continuous improvement projects was presented as a consideration for promotion and higher pay.

- It was not mandatory for supervisors to complete projects.
- Only certain supervisors that had the skill and desire completed projects.
- Supervisors' motivation could have been to make their environment better, give evidence for possible promotion, or earn a pay raise—it didn't matter.
- That individuals had an option to complete projects presented an opportunity for the employer to identify high performers and see who wanted to advance his or her career and contribute in a larger way.
- Supervisors and teams did have a CI manager to help coach them.

Advanced Thinking—Preparing for Chapter 6

Based on my experience in supervisory positions, I have found that many supervisors spend a lot of their time with employees who are "difficult," e.g., not always performing to their abilities, but worse…showing an attitude, treating others badly, choosing not to follow rules, etc. One of the key things I learned over time was about "people treatment." Specifically, how you treat people matters, and it is critical that you avoid being quick to judge, and you can't take things personally. There is very little room for emotion in manufacturing. Emotions potentially risk safety!

To be a successful supervisor, restraint is critical. You have to wait to gather the data and get the facts before making judgments and usually this applies to decision-making too. Learning to listen and be a conscientious observer is very important.

What do you think?

CHAPTER 6

AEIOU—the Masotti Method for Assessment and Observation

Almost all quality improvement comes via simplification of design, manufacturing, layout, processes, and procedures.

—Tom Peters

Based on my work supporting workplace civility initiatives, I have come to understand that one of the measures of success for any workplace civility initiative is the extent to which employees (at all levels) **transfer** what they learn in training or through on-the-job coaching to their day-to-day work. No amount of good intentions, no amount of brilliant training, and no amount of organizational goal setting will be of value if the employees don't change how they speak, and think, and treat each other. This is why a critical aspect of any workplace change ties to the second prong/step in the Trident Approach which is assessment and observation. This step is important for identifying initial training needs, but also crucial for measuring improvement and change.

A **needs assessment** is a systematic exploration of the way things are and the way they should be. These "things" are usually associated with organizational and/or individual performance.

The purpose of conducting a needs assessment is to better understand the reason why things are the way they are—rather than the way they should be and/or how we want them to be. Analyzing the issues and factors that are creating the current situation helps us know what the solution is to get us where we want to be, and where, when, and how we will apply that solution.

We often make assumptions about the reason for things being how they are, and this can result in costly mistakes. For example, if we automatically assume that low productivity in a manufacturing context is due to a lack of employee competence, we might spend a lot of time and money delivering training, only to discover that the problem wasn't competence at all. Maybe the problem was in fact outdated equipment or internal systems. Given the speed of change and the cost of these mistakes, organizations simply cannot afford to make rash decisions—needs assessment is an effective way to control some of the investment costs of change.

Assessment for workplace training may include assessing one or all of the following:

- The organization (in its entirety or one or more departments, or divisions)
- The team(s)
- Or the individual(s)

One of the key reasons a needs assessment is completed prior to launching a change initiative or training plan is to manage resources. Training takes time and money and so it just makes sense to have an idea what you are training, why you are training, and who needs the training *before* you train.

There are many additional benefits to completing a needs assessment. These include increased ability to:

- Focus the training on what's important at a specific time for a specific learner
- Identify strengths and weaknesses of learners
- Identify continuous improvements to current structure
- Fit learning to learner
- Identify a future learning path
- Fit trainer to the need of the learner
- Identify metrics by which to measure success
- Align gaps in goals
- Build a framework for a training communication plan
- Establish expectations for return on investment

- Assess engagement
- Identify risks
- Build a frame of reference
- Enable priorities for action to be established
- Plan the most effective development of limited resources, for instance, to ensure cost effectiveness and value for money
- Justify investment in training by showing how it will contribute to achieving corporate objectives
- Provide a basis for integrating training into the business by getting line management involvement and commitment

There are two typical approaches to completing a workplace civility assessment:

1. Helping people identify performance issues—consider what skills gaps are causing the issues as well as how planned training can help to solve them.
2. Taking a big picture view of the whole organization—consider current, present, and future activities and goals, and then develop training plans to meet the identified current and anticipated training needs.

Depending on the outcomes you are looking for, you will choose either #1 or #2. For example, if your primary issue is attrition and your goal is retention, you might consider starting with #2. If your issue is a specific employee or group of employees who are not working well together, you might start with #1.

With civility initiatives, because we can often identify elements of overall workplace culture as causing incivility at work, we typically recommend starting with an organizational culture assessment.

It is always recommended that you use a combination of several needs assessment methods including:

- Direct observation
- Questionnaires
- Consultation with persons in key positions, and/or with specific knowledge

- Review of relevant literature
- Interviews
- Focus groups
- Tests
- Records and report studies
- Work samples

While it is understood that identifying a key issue or problem (or more than one) that the organization is looking to address with a civility solution is in fact part of assessment, we consider it to be more of an awareness-raising exercise for the organization. However, the data collected in completing this pre-work is used to inform the next steps which we consider to be the "formal" assessment, or in the case of manufacturing environments, on-the-job assessment which happens by way of observation.

One of the Masotti methods is a new approach to observation on the job, specific to manufacturing. The method is called AEIOU.

A

Assess performance and approach the employee. This applies to both positive performance and unsatisfactory performance. If it is evident that the employee is not completing a task as required or there are performance issues related to SOPs or job description, you need to approach the employee to address the issue but be mindful not to focus only on negative performance. It is crucial that there is equal recognition of positive and negative performance. This builds trust and credibility. Choose a "cool" or neutral time, e.g., do not approach an individual during a shift change, break, at the beginning of a shift, or during a stressful period. A good time is usually as the employee is returning from a break. Ensure coverage and ask to speak to the employee in a neutral area that is reasonably private. Show by your demeanor and expressions, that your approach isn't punishment or stressful.

E

Regardless of whether performance is positive or negative, *engage and evaluate* each SOP once a month with the employee. This is essentially a task audit to ensure SOP is effective on an ongoing basis. Make changes as necessary based on feedback and discussion with the employee. Ask questions as you review the SOP line by line. Ideally, you are making an approach to give positive feedback and/or to build trust and facilitate communication; however, if you have to give constructive feedback or require corrective action, use the Masotti feedback method (see Chapter 7).

I

Involve the employee. Ensure you offer opportunities for employees to provide input. Listen patiently, take notes, and encourage employee to ask questions and share ideas and information. Actively create opportunities for the employee to become part of the process. Ask if they need additional tools, supports, training, etc. Be open-minded and go into the situation expecting to listen more than talk. Don't make assumptions and be open to discussions on topics or issues that may not have been part of your initial intention or plan when you first approached the employee. Make adjustments to the SOP that includes employee input where applicable and appropriate. Thank the employee for his or her contribution.

O

Observe the employee after the feedback is delivered. Using your social intelligence skills, watch for cues that he or she has received the feedback positively and is sufficiently comfortable to go back to work.

U

Upskill...that is, provide and address (as soon as possible) any additional tools, supports, training, or other requests the employee requested, particularly if they relate directly to the SOP and/or tasks the employee is required to complete. The timeliness of these upskill responses are critical to building and maintaining trust with the employee.

On the surface, the AEIOU method might seem simple enough. However, to use it, there are aspects which leaders who come from, or work in, traditional command and control manufacturing environments might struggle with.

Under the "A" (assess) leaders sometimes shy away from engaging in neutral or positive interactions, as doing so might be perceived as weak or overly friendly or even coddling behaviour. Or, some leaders might avoid giving bad news or engaging in corrective actions and so they are more focused on making friends with employees. This can be a costly mistake. At the end of the day, it is okay for leaders to be friendly, but it is important to always maintain credibility. Employees need to know their supervisors and managers are competent and can be trusted to make decisions. In a crisis, it is trust and credibility that ensure teams follow directions.

Under the "E," it is important that SOPs be reviewed on a regular and consistent basis. It is going to be very difficult to give feedback to employees—especially if you need to correct a behaviour—if the SOP documents are out of date. Many organizations recognize this, but over the course of day-to-day activities, priorities shift and when a supervisory "to do" item has to be dropped off the list, one of the first things to be neglected is the SOP review.

Under the "I," for it to work well, observation is actually a two-way activity. To be effective, supervisors must listen and observe with their ears as well as their eyes, they have to wait for responses when they ask questions, and they need to be deliberate in involving the employee in the process. The employee will be observing the supervisor too, so the supervisor should be acutely aware of his or her own nonverbal and tonal cues, the power of words, and overall tone.

Under the "O," observation is an ongoing process. And sometimes it is effective not to have a specific list of cues or signals that you are watching for. With gender, generational, and cultural diversity in the workplace, leaders have to have high social acuity. They need to be able to adjust their own social approach and style, and they need to be able to pick up on and effectively interpret the nonverbal cues of a diverse employee pool.

And lastly, under the "U," leaders have to understand that their job is not complete until they have followed through on observations. It is critical that responses to requests, disciplinary actions, and even promises related to positive aspects of performance are completed as quickly as possible. This is an important trust-builder.

For Review

With regard to observation, many leaders make the mistake of paying attention after the fact, that is, after the error, the crisis, the safety issue etc. This is a reactionary approach that can cost time, money, and energy.

When leaders are in the habit (and it does take training for observation to become a habit) of observation, assessment is proactive and preventative.

When you do an observation, you can:

- Identify risks
- Explain the tasks
- Make sure the employee understands the purpose of assessment
- Make sure the employee understands his or her accountability

However, if you have a poor relationship with team members, observation—ongoing, random, or even scheduled—can be perceived as the supervisor looking for errors. When there is little trust between the parties, people tend to assume the worst of each other.

One of the challenges supervisors and managers face is overriding a culture of fear and/or navigating rifts between management and the production floor. This culture of fear and tension is due in part to how historically supervisors are often only told to complete observations on the heels of an injury or error or complaint. For this reason, every time a supervisor approaches a production team member, that employee anticipates the worst. He or she might be nervous or stressed or defensive for no reason except a perception that the only reason supervisors come around is to make the employee's life difficult or because there is a problem.

One easy way to offset some of the fear and tension is to let employees know when and why they are being observed. This approach is often written as policy when workplaces decide to embed civility into best practices. In this way, employees are not caught off guard and don't feel as stressed or worry that they can't protect themselves if something unexpected happens. When observation is treated like a "normal" exchange or interaction between an employee and supervisor, this can be a trust-builder. The overall mood of the communication becomes more positive because it is perceived by both sides as a legitimate way to learn and make necessary changes, and to support the team and activities. In addition, the power balance is less skewed to the supervisor and so shared more equally with the employee. Having said all that, when a leader is very skilled at conducting assessments, the employee frequently won't even know he or she is being assessed. This is an ideal scenario as you will more likely observe typical behavior versus staged behavior.

Sometimes what was intended as an opportunity to observe an employee on the job becomes just about making contact. It is an opportunity to interact and build rapport. However, seasoned supervisors can be observing informally during these types of interactions. He or she can look for:

- What the employee is wearing, e.g., personal protection equipment
- Demeanor and body language, e.g., nervous
- Cleanliness of station
- Overall effort to interact, which can be an indicator of trust and morale—do they seem rushed?
- General mood, e.g., does the employee look frustrated? Or ill? Tired?

When supervisors have high social intelligence, one of the outcomes is that their social radar is accurate. Being able to pick up on nonverbal cues in environments where there is a lot of noise and distraction and/or where for a range of reasons, employees might not vocalize much, being able to read body language accurately can be a tremendous benefit. Some common cues and their meaning are shared here:

Signs that you have someone's attention:

- Smiling
- Nodding
- Eyebrows raised
- Saying, "Yes, please go on…"
- Leaning forward
- He or she is actively listening
- He or she is so excited to talk to you that they interrupt or finish your sentences

Signs that someone is losing interest:

- His or her eyes are wandering, looking over your shoulder, not making eye contact, looking down or at their watch
- Fidgeting
- Pursed lips or closed mouth smile
- He or she is whispering or doing something other than listening to you
- Yawning or stretching
- He or she interrupts you or changes the subject

Signs that someone is uncomfortable or feeling awkward:

- Pacing
- Rising or shifting away from you
- Leaving the area or room completely
- Fidgeting
- Head lowered, no eye contact
- Shoulders rounded, closed posture
- Blushing
- Profuse sweating
- Trembling
- Complaints of nausea or headache or just not looking as though they feel good
- Talking too much or not at all
- Not eating or drinking or just eating and/or drinking

Signs that someone does not believe you or is not "buying in":

- Repeating themselves, saying, "yeah, yeah…." or "sure, sure, okay…yeah"
- He or she is saying "yes" with their mouth but their body language says "no"
- Not asking any questions at all, signaling that they've already made up their minds
- Arms crossed

Signs that someone is not being entirely honest:

- Changes in the voice's pitch, rate of speech, or volume of speech
- Hesitation(s) when speaking
- Decreased or increased eye contact
- Hands moving to cover the eyes or mouth
- Nervous movements of hands, feet, or legs; twitching of eye
- Saying things that don't make sense or suddenly changing the subject

Watch for these clues and cues before taking the spoken word as fact. Make a mental note of the gestures, eye contact, facial expressions, and the other person's respect for your personal space. Comments and feedback may need to be based on additional information if there is a question of understanding or conflicting messages. Remember to ask questions to clarify when you are not quite sure or need more information before responding or making a decision. With the majority of the message (55 percent) having a considerable effect on the message, take the time to learn and study nonverbal communication and most importantly be careful when communicating your own messages.

During observation sessions, supervisors can ask straightforward questions. If the supervisor waits and listens, the answers to these questions can provide a lot of information.

Examples of general question:

- How can things be better?
- Do you see any risks?
- Do you feel you need more training?
- Do you think you can do this job effectively with the tools you have?
- Do you think we have the proper tools?
- Have you read the updated SOP?
- Do you understand the job description? Or do you understand the elements of the job?

Regardless of the timing or purpose of the observation and assessment, supervisors who learn and acknowledge that treating people well all day, and every day, will have significantly easier interactions with their employees. The problem is that many supervisors do not engage in positive people treatment. For example, managers might tell a new supervisor to "build rapport" or "encourage your team to collaborate" or "get them to trust you," etc., but the fact is the supervisor simply does not have the skills or knowledge to do these things.

Over 20+ years in the field, the field team at Civility Experts Inc. have devised a list of behaviors that constitute positive people treatment. To build trust with their teams, ALL leaders, at all levels, need to be trained in positive people treatment behaviors and they need to consistently model those behaviors on the job.

People Treatment Self-Assessment
By L. Bayer, Civility Experts Inc. All rights reserved.

☐ Posture, e.g., I present myself (physically) as open-minded, ready to engage, and approachable

☐ Time management, e.g., I show that I understand time is a valuable resource, e.g., don't waste my time or time of others, be on time

☐ Expectations, e.g., have clear expectations for oneself and for others

☐ Treat people fairly, e.g., equal opportunity, use same criteria to measure equally, etc.

☐ Honesty, e.g., be honest, tell the whole truth whenever possible

☐ Tone, e.g., I consider tonal elements when I interact verbally with others including:
  ○ Pace
  ○ Word choice
  ○ Volume
  ○ Timing
  ○ Privacy/confidentiality
  ○ Emotionality
  ○ Impact
  ○ Relationship, e.g., accountability and familiarity
  ○ Cultural nuances
  ○ Risk, e.g., perceptions related to gender
  ○ Expectations of listener, e.g., generational aspects
  ○ Mode of communication, e.g., face to face, phone, etc.

☐ Indication of bias, e.g.: Am I aware that I change my approach depending on who I am interacting with?

☐ Common courtesy, e.g., eye contact, handshake, proximity, smile, introductions, please, thank you, offering food or beverage, etc.

☐ Care with word choice, e.g., consider frame of reference

☐ Perspectives on role, rank, status, and contribution

Figure 12 Positive People Treatment Self-Assessment©, Civility Experts Inc. 2018

- Communication approach, e.g., formal versus informal, conversational versus legal, personal versus professional
- Willingness to adapt to individual need, e.g., if someone needs support due to physical or physiological barriers
- Perception of differences, e.g.: Do I see differences as advantages or as barriers?
- Ability to show respect, e.g., by interacting in a way that leaves the other person feeling valued (I understand that respect is not something people need to earn; we are all deserving of respect because we are human beings)
- Ability to build rapport, e.g., ease and flow of interaction
- Response in stressful or emotional settings, e.g.: Do I stay calm? Do I help others be calm? Can I exercise restraint?
- Ability to build trust and to be perceived as trustworthy
- Openness, e.g., authenticity and vulnerability
- Ability to effectively interpret verbal, nonverbal, tonal, and contextual cues
- Situational awareness, e.g., recognize factors that might impact people
- Ability to adapt social style appropriately
- Cultural competence, e.g., recognize, adapt, and work with differences
- Emotional intelligence, e.g., be aware of my own issues and hot buttons
- Ability to empathize and share perspective
- Ego, e.g., attitude about one's own importance
- Humility, e.g., ability to acknowledge gifts and contributions of others over focusing on one's own gifts, talents, and contributions
- Willingness to learn
- Patience, e.g., to listen
- Willingness to apologize
- Curiosity, e.g., interest in learning and asking questions
- Readiness to forgive, e.g., accept apologies with grace
- Recognition of human condition, e.g., acknowledge that I can't always understand or know what another person is experiencing
- Generosity, e.g., ability to give with no expectation of return
- Systems thinking, e.g., ability to consider impact of actions and decisions
- Social acuity, e.g., ability to assess and interpret interpersonal connections and cost, benefits, and consequences of the same
- Values, e.g.: Can I articulate my values if necessary, and do I live my values?
- Ability to acknowledge and celebrate achievements and contributions of others
- Positive attitude, e.g., look for the best in people and in situations
- Responsibility, e.g., take care of myself, don't blame others or expect others to manage me (my daily life or actions or activities)
- Accountability, e.g., own my own tasks and decisions
- Service orientation, e.g.: Do I show through my actions that I am "other-focused" and can put the needs of others before my own needs and wants when appropriate or required?

Figure 12 Continued

When you treat people well, and build trust, an additional measurable outcome is **relational wealth**. One of the key measurable benefits of civility anywhere—but particularly in the workplace—is the positive impact on relational wealth. As per Civility Experts Inc. definition, "relational wealth" is a quantifiable level—or sense of—meaning attributed to the value (especially when perceived as positive) of an interpersonal relationship.

This definition is adapted from an article by Roeish Diwan published in July 2000 in the *Journal on Social Economics*. According to Diwan, relational wealth is derived from, and deeply rooted in, family and community values.

It is possible to measure relational wealth, and then, based on the measurements, adjust behaviour such that we can increase it. On the Bayer Relational Value Chart© you can see that there are two axes for measuring value:

- Level of reliance on the relationship/interaction
  This refers to the extent to which a person truly needs another person/connection/relationship. For example, is there high reliance due to:
  - Financial dependence?
  - Emotional security?
  - Power imbalance, i.e., one person is the other's boss, parent, or other authority?
  - Physical dependence, i.e., one person cannot manage independently, e.g., is special abled, elderly, young, or incapacitated in some way
  The more an individual needs another, the higher the reliance. The less an individual needs another, the lower the reliance.
- Quality of the relationship/interaction
  This refers to the extent to which the interaction/connection/relationship adds value (or in civility language, eases the experience) to another. For example, does interacting with this person:
  - Provide happiness?
  - Offer emotional support?
  - Improve quality of life?
  The more benefit there is to the relationship, without overt or less obvious cost to the benefitting individual, the higher the quality of the relationship is assessed to be. The less benefit, and more cost, to the benefitting individual, the lower the quality of the relationship is perceived to be.

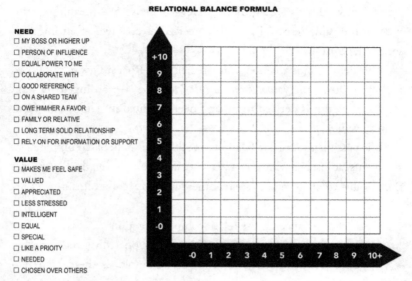

Figure 13 Relational Wealth Grid©, Civility Experts Inc. 2018

As you can see from the chart, a high need/high quality relationship is going to score high on relational value. Similarly, a low need/low quality relationship is going to score low on relational value. It is also important to consider power dynamics and trust—when two people are involved in a high need/high quality relationship, and where the scores are close for both parties, there is mutual respect and trust. However, if one person scores the relationship with high need and the other does not, it is likely that there is low trust on one side and there will be an imbalance in the quality of the relationship as experienced by each of the individuals.

There should also be some consideration for relationships where both parties score the interactions as low need, but high quality, for example, friends who add value to each other's lives but who could manage well enough without each other if necessary.

When we look at workplace relationships, it is important to consider relational wealth scores when there is incivility because uncivil attitudes and actions can frequently be attributed to low trust. Often the "need" in workplace relationships is based on power, e.g., the need to earn a wage or garner favor or keep a job. This high need can cause individuals to tolerate poor quality interactions because they don't feel they have an option.

With regard to reliance, people can miss opportunities or put a different (misunderstood) value on people based on various criteria. This can result in missed opportunities.

For example, most people would put a boss at a 10 for need. But for quality of interaction, they might give a low score, let's say a 2.

The higher position or power a person has in a company, the more people tend to assume a high need. BUT, if I only see that person four times a year, does he or she really have that much impact or influence over me?

In addition, we may undervalue people we interact with regularly who have more influence and upon whom we have higher reliance than we perceive. We need to also consider the frequency of interaction as well as the interdependence of the various relationships we are involved in.

Some examples are:

- On a sports team, you might think the general manager or head coach are the highest need relationships. BUT, you actually have more meaningful interactions with your position coach, and one of the people you should be valuing more is the equipment manager—he or she actually has significant influence and power over you, by ensuring you are safe and have the equipment you need to do your job well.
- If you are a supervisor on a manufacturing floor, you might be inclined to rank your manager as high need. This is potentially a mistake. Every day, sometimes three times a day, most supervisors write an e-mail report (basically a performance review) and send it out to everyone on the leadership team. The report includes data and key metrics that are shared with others at the supervisor's peer level and higher-ups. (e.g., plant manager, etc.) Everyone is commenting and sharing and learning from these reports. What often happens is when supervisors get promoted, they tend to suddenly stop sharing these reports with other supervisors, and only value the next level up. In disregarding or undervaluing the lower leadership levels, you have just dismissed and undermined the people you manage—the people who do the work and can actually make your job easier.

Who will help you more? The three or four leaders at levels over you? Or, as in the case of a manufacturing plant, the 50 to 60 people on the line who actually do the work that you, in theory, are accountable for? The team you support are the people who can impact the quality of your day-to-day work experience.

In filling in the relational wealth grid, it is extremely important to be honest about where/how you score people. And then, look at the chart with a critical eye and ask:

A) When you look at "quality" of the relationship, consider aspects such as:
   - Does my involvement in this relationship benefit me personally but cause strife or issue with others, e.g., do I have to choose between relationships?
   - Is the quality predictable or consistent? For example, a one-time benefit or aspect of quality that is fleeting or inconsistent may actually be overvalued when you look at the long-term cost.

If you value the wrong relationships and kowtow to people who you perceive as beneficial, but you are actually incorrect or misperceiving the quality of those interactions, you are possibly misplacing your attention and energy. In addition, you risk losing trust and being perceived as a "low need" by those around you that you interact with every day. In manufacturing, this can impact safety because the people around me think I don't care about them, so they don't care about me.

- Union representative versus lead hand?
- Parent versus friend?
- Pastor at church versus grandparent?
- Softball coach versus teammates?
- University professor versus new friend/student in class?
- Doctor versus favorite aunt?
- Manager versus coworker?
- Admin person versus veteran employee?
- President versus local city councilor?
- Plant manager versus line team?
- Celebrity spokesperson versus sister who tried the product firsthand?
- Google search versus personal experience?

You should consider increasing your perceived need of the people you work most closely with and/or interact with every day.

From a civility point of view, an important understanding is that EVERYONE HAS VALUE. This is the crux of Civility Experts Inc.'s entire philosophy. When you acknowledge and truly believe that each individual has something to contribute and that each person is deserving of respect—that being respected at a basic human level is not something people need to earn—how you treat people changes.

It's when you encounter off-standard conditions that relational wealth scores become most meaningful.

You can have a set of rules and a job description and ask people to follow it. And you can be an "arms-length" supervisor, in that you are technically doing your job, but you are not building trust or rapport, or connecting with people on a humankind level.

However, if you make the effort to show that you value people, you can balance the scale because the people who report to you see that you need them too. The power balance is closer aligned.

Employees will perform in off-standard conditions and, in fact, often the off-standard condition goes unnoticed or is resolved almost seamlessly because the people who feel valued, like and trust you and so they just manage themselves and manage small issues and will step out of their job description, anticipate issues, or give you information to prevent potential problems before they happen.

What is interesting in manufacturing is that supervisors, managers, continuous improvement personnel, various lean consultants, etc. actually need there to be real issues and problems so that they can solve them. The issue is that you can't use these strategies until after the problem has occurred because that's where the data comes from. Kaizen and **Six Sigma** and other similar **DMAIC** approaches are all after-the-fact solutions. Sure, they work, but at what cost? The problems and issues should never happen in the first place.

With civility as best practice, we would follow the exact same process, BUT, we gather the data proactively AND it didn't cost us anything. And this is true of safety metrics too. If an employee feels psychologically safe and comfortable telling you he or she is not feeling safe to do his or her job, this is a GOOD thing!

The way you get data and information about problems that haven't happened yet is by building relationships. If employees see their supervisor as high value, they are more likely to share information.

When positive people treatment happens on an ongoing basis and particularly at the assessment and observation stages, continuous improvement, and corrective action happens before the incident/event even happens. Do we celebrate that we put stops and fixes in place AFTER an employee loses his hand? Or do we want to celebrate that no employee loses his hand because we put the stops and fixes in place BEFORE an accident happens?

Relational wealth is a factor of perceived need, quality of interaction, and at work, quantity of interaction is also important.

Key Takeaways

- Don't risk a missed opportunity by undervaluing the people that you interact with the most.
- Collect data on events that haven't happened yet, versus collecting data on events after they happened.
- Relational wealth is the difference between a good and a great supervisor, e.g., a civil supervisor will outperform anyone when off-standard conditions happen.
- Anyone can run the place when things are going well. But when things go off track, that's when you will see the benefit of building relational wealth.
- The biggest opportunity to develop relational wealth is with the people you interact with the most.
- Building relational wealth is a precursor to continuous improvement as you are fixing something before it happens.
- Relational wealth has a direct positive impact on when you encounter off-standard conditions.

Homework Assignment

Listed below are two situations where a supervisor/manager has to ask questions because what might seem like the situation on the surface is

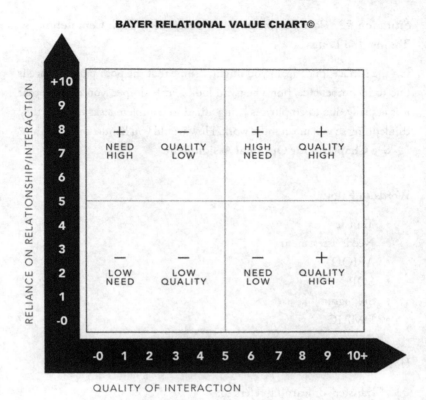

Figure 14 Relational Value Chart©, Civility Experts Inc. 2018

actually not as simple as it seems, i.e., he or she cannot be quick to judge or assess the situation.

Review the situations and answer the questions.

Situation #1: Poor Performance—Specifically, Employee Is Just Not Completing the Work

On the surface, you might assume the poor performance is due to incompetence, but when you look a little deeper you observe that it is actually due to peer pressure. How would you handle this situation?

Situation #2: Poor Performance—Specifically, Task Completion Is Taking Too Long

On the surface, once again you might assume that the poor performance is due to incompetence, but when you look a little deeper, you observe that it is actually due to employees being afraid to complete tasks because they think doing so will mean more work. How would you handle this situation?

See Chapter 9 for Optional Assignment.

Words to Know

- Transfer
- Needs assessment
- AEIOU
- SOP
- Six Sigma
- DMAIC

How Much Do You Remember?

1. "Transfer" of learning refers to:
    a. Sharing what you know with someone else
    b. Using what you learn on the job
    c. Mentoring
    d. Using skills from one job at the next job
2. If you are speaking to someone and his or her eyes start to wander, he or she looks away or lowers his or her head, this may be a sign that the person:
    a. is disappointed
    b. is disinterested
    c. is distracted
    d. does not like you
3. The main purpose of an assessment is to:
    a. understand why things are how they are
    b. identify how things should be
    c. figure out what needs to be changed
    d. sort employees based on competency

4. A good time to assess employee performance is:
   a. when employee is on a short, scheduled break
   b. before or after regular scheduled work hours
   c. when employee is just finishing break
   d. during employee's lunch period

Recommended Reading

Greensteen, L.M. 2012. *Assessing 21st Century Skills: A Guide to Evaluating Mastery and Authentic Learning.* Thousand Oaks, CA: Corwin Press.

Advanced Thinking—Preparing for Chapter 7

Based on my experience in supervisory positions, I have found that many supervisors spend a lot of their time with employees who are "difficult," e.g., not always performing to their abilities, but worse…showing an attitude, treating others badly, choosing not to follow rules, etc. One of the key things I learned over time was about "people treatment." Specifically, how you treat people matters. It is critical that you avoid being quick to judge, and you can't take things personally. There is very little room for emotion in manufacturing. Emotions pose a potential safety risk.

To be a successful supervisor, restraint is critical. You have to stay calm, wait to gather the data, and get the facts before making judgments and usually this applies to decision-making too. Learning to listen and being a conscientious observer is very important.

What do you think?

CHAPTER 7

The Masotti Methods

What get measured, gets managed.
—Peter Drucker

One of the challenges manufacturing and union-based organizations face is building and maintaining a positive culture in environments that are historically competitive, process-driven, and perceived by many to be inhumane, e.g., by way of an assertive management style, disciplinary focus, and often a divisive mentality between management and front line. In these environments, day-to-day communication can be difficult. Day-to-day management of production activities can be difficult. And implementing change can be difficult. It's all difficult a lot of the time—but it's not impossible.

Over the last 20 years, I have worked in a range of organizations, including various auto manufacturing plants, (Ford, Chrysler, Toyota) as well as food and wine manufacturers. Among other positions, I have also been a customer service advisor for a Cadillac dealership and for Freightlighner, and a Maintenance Supervisor at Bombardier.

At the time of writing this book, I work part-time in sports as a conversions supervisor for Maple Leaf Sports & Entertainment, (Raptors, Toronto Maple Leafs). I'm telling you this because success in conversions is about managing the people who implement the processes of changing over the venue. In many ways, it's no different than managing the people who manage the processes in a manufacturing plant. I've had personal success in both environments, due in part to some communication habits of mine, that my colleagues at Civility Experts Inc. have now labeled "the Masotti Methods."

Generally, the benefits of incorporating civility into manufacturing policies and practices are many, including:

- Reworking organizational policy that may in fact be encouraging and fostering incivility and inhumane practices
- Eliminating of time spent on disciplinary and corrective paperwork
- Fostering a culture of learning versus a culture of fear
- Building skills that eliminate defects and rework (**MUDA**)
- Utilizing communication strategies that result in collaboration, civility, and clarity
- Instilling practices for documentation that are concise, accurate, and civil
- Reducing tension between leadership/management and employees

The Masotti methods are three specific techniques that make up "prong 3" or the third step in the Trident Approach. The Trident Approach (introduced in Chapter 3) is an intervention strategy for changing workplace culture via behavior and mindset shift. The first of the three Masotti methods for civil communication at work is the AEIOU Approach covered in Chapter 6. Second is the Masotti feedback method which is discussed here in Chapter 7. And the "make the box smaller" method is addressed in Chapter 8. Each method addresses specific ways to incorporate civility into workplace best practices related to communication. Doing so makes day-to-day communication, management, and change all less difficult.

In manufacturing environments where optimization and efficiency are key business goals, and where achieving these goals requires strict adherence to safety and quality guidelines, **feedback** is a critical communication tool.

In addition to providing a means for conveying information, feedback offers an opportunity for relationship building, tracking progress, and problem-solving.

For employees, receiving effective feedback promotes personal and professional growth. And for leaders, feedback is about listening actively, taking the time to analyze, and then thinking of the best possible solution to perform better. When done well, feedback provides positive criticism and allows everyone to see what they can change to improve their focus and results.[1]

Unfortunately, many supervisors and managers underestimate the need for, and impact of, feedback. This is a mistake. You may not know it, but companies who implement regular employee feedback have turnover rates that are 14.9 percent lower than for employees who receive no feedback.[2]

In addition, only 14.5 percent of managers strongly agree that they are effective at giving feedback.[3] This self-assessment is accurate because over the past 40 years psychometricians have shown in study after study that people don't have the objectivity to hold in their heads a stable definition of an abstract quality, such as *business acumen* or *assertiveness*, and then accurately evaluate someone else on it. Our evaluations are deeply colored by our own understanding of what we're rating others on, our own sense of what good looks like for a particular competency, our harshness or leniency as raters, and our own inherent and unconscious biases. This phenomenon is called the **idiosyncratic rater effect**, and it's large (more than half of your rating of someone else reflects your characteristics, not hers) and resilient (no training can lessen it). In other words, the research shows that feedback is more distortion than truth. The research also shows that focusing people on their shortcomings or gaps doesn't enable learning. It impairs it.[4] Sadly, the majority of feedback conversations focus on highlighting what isn't being done well. As such, only 26 percent of

---

[1] actiTIME. March, 2018. "The Importance of Feedback." www.actitime.com/project-management/importance-of-feedback/. 04/08/2019

[2] M.D. Photiades. July 2, 2014. "6 Eye-Opening Employee Engagement Statistics," *TalentCulture*. https://talentculture.com/6-eye-opening-employee-engagement-statistics/. 02/12/2018

[3] C. Brower, and N. Dvorak. October 11, 2019. "Why Employees Are Fed Up with Feedback," *Gallup.com*. www.gallup.com/workplace/267251/why-employees-fed-feedback.aspx (accessed May 14, 2020). 05/05/2020

[4] M. Buckingham, and A. Goodall. September 17, 2019. "Why Feedback Rarely Does What It's Meant To," *Harvard Business Review*. https://hbr.org/2019/03/the-feedback-fallacy#:~:text=Managers%20today%20are%20bombarded%20with,in%20fact%2C%20can%20hinder%20development.

employees say the feedback they receive improves their work. And, shockingly, four out of five employees who received negative feedback are job hunting.[5]

The Masotti Feedback Method is a unique approach to managing potentially difficult, complex, or crucial conversations, by way of utilizing civility in a systematic and strategic way. In addition to improving rapport, diminishing potential conflict, and building trust, using this approach increases an organization's ability to align the business priorities with its organizational values. This results in high-performance work environments and high accountability. In addition, supervisors and managers who consistently adopt this feedback approach will find themselves acting proactively versus reactively. They will be better managers in terms of meeting output objectives while concurrently fostering trust, respect, and humanity at work.

Delivering feedback using this Masotti method also benefits individual employees in the following ways:

- Makes their jobs easier
- Helps them save time
- Builds trust with colleagues and higher-ups
- Increases likelihood that employee will feel comfortable asking for feedback
- Eases communication
- Reduces stress
- Fosters collaboration and cooperation
- Supports a culture of learning
- Helps separate facts from feelings, i.e., effective feedback is fact-based

While giving feedback is not new, the way I suggest supervisors and managers give feedback is innovative because the approach considers:

a) Behavior triggers, e.g., fear, culture, labels, and habits (of both the person giving and the person receiving feedback)

---

[5]C. Musser. December 20, 2019. "The Most Effective Feedback Is the Kind You Ask for," *Gallup.com*. www.gallup.com/workplace/271184/effective-feedback-kind-ask .aspx (accessed May 14, 2020).

b) Consequences, e.g., extent to which individuals are held accountable for behavior
c) Assumptions and unconscious bias, e.g., this is how we do it here
d) Measurable, quantifiable behaviors and outcomes
e) Tone and experience, e.g., the communicator initiating the interaction determines the overall experience

The strategy is best applied as an intervention tool. You would use the approach when:

- You observe errors on the floor, i.e., through a job observation—you use the intervention strategy BEFORE you engage in corrective action
- You hear or observe miscommunications that potentially impact safety, production, quality, or cost—you use the intervention strategy BEFORE you engage in repetitive and/or ineffective communication, in print, or orally
- You observe positive behavior—you would use the strategy as soon as you observe the behavior

So here is how the Masotti Feedback Method works:

Step 1: **Build rapport and trust on an ongoing basis.** Supervisors and managers should anticipate that they will be required to provide ongoing feedback to everyone they supervise. And they should anticipate having to give feedback when things are going well as well as when there are issues or challenges. To mitigate the perceived stress that often accompanies feedback interactions, leaders should learn to communicate with civility and engage in ongoing positive people treatment. By doing this, they will build trust and rapport and will find it easier to gather data and assess performance informally and with increased cooperation. When there is a good rapport, employees are less threatened by being assessed and observed. They come to see it as an opportunity to improve the workplace overall, to find ways to make their job and the job of their colleagues easier and safer, and they come to see the supervisor as a colleague who is working towards the same goals versus someone trying to catch them doing something wrong. Supervisors can build trust by consistently exhibiting positive people treatment behavior (see Chapter 6) as well as by doing the following:

○ THINK FIRST: Is feedback required? If the behavior doesn't impact you, the team, or the organization in a specific and meaningful way, consider whether you need to address it. If you need to give feedback, concentrate on the behavior versus worrying about the person exhibiting the behavior—this helps you observe actions or words—and try not to label or fall back on your own opinions or personal feelings about the individual. Initially, you need not be concerned about "why" the employee is behaving in a certain way; that is, don't speculate or assume you understand his or her motivation. Specifically, how he or she feels isn't necessarily relevant. But you do care about the "why" related to behavior, for example:

- Why isn't he or she doing what is on the SOP or job description?
- Why isn't he or she asking for help?
- How long has the behavior been going on?
- What can you actually see and measure? Stick to the facts.

○ IDENTIFY CONSEQUENCES, e.g., in the case of corrective action. To be meaningful, consequences should:

- Impact the employee/individual in a meaningful way, e.g., cause some discomfort or disparity
- Be timely, e.g., within minutes of the inappropriate behavior being observed
- Should be definite, e.g., not threatened or delayed, you have to follow through

○ REMEMBER THE BIG PICTURE: Good supervisors understand that the goal is to move the *whole* group along the performance continuum. Even incremental movement forward can have significant impacts. Give feedback to all employees. Often, we don't give time or attention to the positive high performers, as we assume they don't need it. But ignoring them and not acknowledging or rewarding them, or at least giving them equal time or attention, can be a demotivator. Or people can become resentful that good performance goes unnoticed. And when a good performer does need you, which isn't often, and you aren't available, this can cause anger or mistrust. Funnily enough, when poor performers see that you are not going to favor them, or that constant negativity or poor performance will not be rewarded, they will often adjust their behavior in a positive way in an effort to get and retain your attention. If, however, you continue to spend the bulk of your time and resources on the 20 percent of poor performers, that group has no incentive to improve. When employees see that every team member will be held to the same standard, it actually builds trust and encourages employees to take personal responsibility for their performance.

○ TAKE A NON-AGGRESSIVE STANCE: When you are giving feedback, be considerate of personal distance, e.g., stand about one arm's length from the employee—not too close to invade his or her personal space, but not so far away that the person has to strain to hear you or gets a sense that you are not really engaging with him or her. Also, employees should always be careful not to get too personal, and to always be sensitive to potential cultural, generational, or gender issues or preferences. Don't touch the other person and try to maintain a friendly but not familiar demeanor.

○ USE SOCIAL RADAR: It is important to observe verbal and nonverbal cues while you are engaging in feedback communications. This might seem like an easy thing to do but many people are uncomfortable about noticing details. This can be for a range of reasons:

- Nervous about being perceived as creepy or that he or she is staring
- Feeling awkward about approaching someone of the opposite sex
- Not in the habit of talking to strangers
- Resistance to change
- Fear of failing or making a mistake
- Fear of being judged by coworkers
- Fear of being rejected by other employees
- Loss of control
- Physical stress
- Low confidence

Step 2: Address supervisor's accountabilities to the employee first. *Before* you consider writing someone up or doing any corrective action you need to ask yourself the following five questions. If you answer "NO" to any of these questions, you should **not** proceed to corrective action:

Q1: Did I (or someone) train this person to do the job?

Sub-questions might include:

- When did I train him or her? Was it some time ago? Has the job or equipment or situation changed?
- If I didn't train him or her, who did? Can I talk to this person?

Q2: Did I document the training? Can I go find out exactly what he or she was taught/told?

Sub-questions might include:

- If I didn't document it, why not?
- What is protocol when I didn't previously document training?

Q3: Did I give specific directions and details? Have expectations been clearly outlined?

Sub-questions might include:

- What directions were given? Do these directions make sense?
- Does he or she have what he needs, e.g., tools, to do what he or she is being asked?

Q4: Did I follow up and check that he or she was doing the job properly and effectively before this issue/challenge arose?

Sub-questions might include:

○ If I didn't follow up, why not?

○ Are there other factors that are contributing to this situation, e.g., a change in policy?

Q5: Did I give him or her effective feedback?

Sub-questions might include:

○ If I didn't, why didn't I?

○ Did someone else give feedback? Is another manager giving different feedback?

○ What was the tone of the feedback?

○ How was the feedback received?

○ How is he or she responding to me? Does it seem that he or she trusts me?

Step 3: Give feedback daily if possible and weekly at a minimum.

The typical process for feedback in manufacturing is to give feedback during periodic job observations, during standard operating procedure reviews, or when a crisis or issue arises. With the Masotti method for feedback, the goal is for supervisors to build relationships with their team such that they are interacting and communicating daily. Giving feedback can take just a few minutes and can be informal. The more at ease employees are being observed, the more likely they will be comfortable asking questions, requesting supports and training, and sharing information on an ongoing basis.

Step 4: Give fact-based, quantifiable feedback.

One of the mistakes most managers/supervisors make when giving feedback is that they are focused on their own feelings and perspective of things. They get emotional, and they lose sight of the end in mind. Or they are too focused on who is doing what, and why he or she is doing it, versus WHAT should be done. The reality is, most often the motives of the action-taker do not matter.

To be effective, feedback must be:

○ Specific—address only one issue at a time

○ Purposeful and targeted, e.g., towards a desired outcome

- Affect something, e.g., influence, change, or redirect
- Behavior-focused, e.g., who is doing it doesn't matter so much as what is being done—BEHAVIOR IS SOMETHING OBSERVABLE, FACT-BASED, and MEASURABLE

A key understanding for the strategy to work is that supervisors and managers MUST have the ability to give feedback in a measured way with a controlled tone. This is an indicator of overall respectfulness, the ability to manage one's emotions (restraint), and personal responsibility. Good leaders understand that you cannot ask other people to speak kindly, manage their emotions, or take personal responsibility unless they (the leaders) can do it themselves. The extent to which feedback is effective is directly related to the credibility of the person providing the feedback. And credibility is achieved in large part through consistency and leading by example.

When giving feedback, supervisors must learn to do the following:

- Wait for responses; don't rush the employee and don't prompt or coerce answers.
- Speak clearly, using conversational language in a fact-based, unemotional way.
- Treat all employees equally.
- When dealing with poor performers, don't assume they don't have the willingness or ability to do better. Rather, focus on discovering why they are not performing at this moment, related to this specific task. There may be a valid reason they are not performing at this time. For example:
  - They don't feel valued.
  - They don't feel physically well.
  - They have personal issues they are dealing with.
  - They are fearful.
  - They don't have the tools they need.
  - They don't know what the expectations are.
  - They need more training.

- ◦ Never ask about the discipline history of a person, and don't solicit opinions from others about the people they work with—this helps avoid bias.
- ◦ Avoid making assumptions. People could perform differently on different shifts, different days, different contexts—you never know what the causal factors are unless you research and ask questions. You have to make your own decision and avoid assumptions and bias.
- ◦ Document the feedback session. You should have already documented data on observation and assessment and now you can add to that information by including questions that are asked, as well as responses.
  - ▪ When documenting observation:
  - ▪ Include facts only
  - ▪ Use measurable language
  - ▪ Record quantitative observations based on set guidelines and procedures

  When reviewing SOPs, discussion should cover:
  - ▪ Roles
  - ▪ Responsibilities
  - ▪ Why the job is important
  - ▪ Urgency of tasks
  - ▪ Timeline
  - ▪ Key indicators, e.g., safety, efficiency, quality
  - ▪ Criticality—level of risk
  - ▪ Steps of how to do the job, e.g., with icons that relate to the criticality of each step
- ◦ Pay attention. For example, you tell an employee you are going through his or her job description and you say, "We are going to go through your job description; if you have any questions or comments stop me."

A top performer possibly responds: "Yes, I understand," or "Thank you, no issues, no questions, I have what I need to do my job."

A poor performer possibly responds: "Wait, I didn't know that," "I don't know how to do that," etc.

NOTE: Even with the best intentions, if a supervisor is not really listening or paying attention, he or she can miss vital cues that actually tell if an employee is in need or not. For example, if I don't look up, but I hear an employee say, "Yeah, I get it, I don't need anything," I might miss the expression or shifting of body weight that actually hints that the employee is uncomfortable or embarrassed or lying. And you need to pay attention to these cues. People will say all kinds of things, but how they act, and what they do is often an indication of what they really feel, think, or know.

It's also important to give people an "out." Let them keep their self-respect and save face. There is no value in diminishing or embarrassing adults at work. For example, if an employee does ask for help, don't chastise him or her.

Let the person come up with a reason why he or she can't do what you need him to her to do. Help them understand that this is a process and that the goal is improvement. Ask, "Do you have any suggestions about...?" Let the individual be part of the process that corrects the problem. Let him or her help relieve the pressure on all sides.

Having said all that—about involving the employee in the process, etc.—the fact is there are times when corrective action will be called for. Sometimes the consequence is defined, e.g., by regulation or policy or union guidelines and so on.

When it comes to safety issues, there is no tolerance or second chances. Further, a determined action is different from behavior. For example, smoking on the job is a behavior. Willfully putting on a wrong part or deliberately ignoring a workplace rule is a **determined action**.

DON'T ASSUME there is malice or some unfounded reason or rationale for a behavior—wait to ask questions and find out the reason. The individual might have a valid point or reason.

ASK WHY the person is engaging in the behavior. Try to start with a root cause approach and try to find out why the person is not performing appropriately.

Here are some examples of behaviors all of which are determined actions and would require corrective action.

1. Putting the wrong taillight on
2. Arguing with a supervisor

3. Smoking in the plant
4. Being drunk or drinking on the job
5. Not wearing safety glasses when working with welding equipment
6. Being 4 minutes late for shift
7. Not doing what he or she was asked to do—e.g., move some steel coils from one part of the plant to another
8. Mistreating another employee, e.g., harassing a coworker
9. Using the incorrect tools
10. Taking a shortcut that will impact quality
11. Deliberately withholding information that will impact someone else negatively (document)
12. Regularly engaging in shop talk or negativity
13. Stealing a piece of equipment or some supplies
14. Failing to interact effectively with coworkers
15. Not doing part of the job for the whole shift (missing parts or tools)

Supervisors must be prepared to outline expectations and provide procedures that make it impossible for people to make mistakes. This information should be relayed during training and in feedback communications.

For Consideration

In the Advanced Thinking section on preparing for Chapter 7, I mentioned that based on my experience in supervisory positions, I have found that many supervisors spend a lot of their time with employees who are "difficult," e.g., not always performing to their abilities, but worse…showing an attitude, treating others badly, choosing not to follow rules, etc. One of the key things I learned over time was about "people treatment." Specifically, how you treat people matters. It is critical that you avoid being quick to judge, and you can't take things personally. There is very little room for emotion in manufacturing. Emotions pose a potential safety risk.

To be a successful supervisor, restraint is critical. You have to stay calm, wait to gather the data and get the facts before making judgments, and usually this applies to decision-making too. Learning to listen and being a conscientious observer is very important. Age, gender, mood, race, experience, job title or task, personality, and even performance—NONE of these are factors that should impact how a supervisor treats others.

Treat everyone the same. This statement can be a hot button. How do you do this? For example:

- Tone of voice
- Process
- Delivery
- Approach
- Questions
- Body language
- Rate of speech
- Word choice
- Assume the best

Exceptions would be when there are special needs; e.g., for an employee who is hearing-impaired, of course you might adjust your speech to accommodate.

Question: Referencing the civility culture continuum chart below, at which stages/levels would you engage in feedback with employees?

Question: How much time should you spend with employees when giving feedback? Do you spend more time when addressing negative behavior?

Question: An employee is sleeping on the job. You catch him. It's a 1-day suspension and he knows that he is caught. How do you manage this situation in a way that changes behavior but builds trust?

For Review

It is important for leaders to remember that concurrent with their assessment and evaluation of their team, their team members are also assessing and evaluating their supervisors and managers. It is critical that supervisors and managers learn to withhold judgment and to be able to restrain themselves, e.g., staying calm regardless of the situation.

There are additional behaviors that supervisors and managers can exhibit to build trust.

The Culture Indicator Continuum

BY MASOTTI & BAYER

Figure 15 Civility Continuum Chart©, Masotti & Bayer 2018

The trick is to avoid varying your responses and behavior based on levels of performance. You want to remove any all real or perceived bias. For example:

- Don't swear or be dramatic or change the volume of your speech when interacting with poor performers.
- Don't be more friendly or cajole and joke or be more light-hearted with high performers.
- Don't physically engage, e.g., shake hands, with some people and not others.
- Don't ignore people or talk behind their back or to a third party (whether good or bad) regardless of performance.
- Don't engage in more personal or social conversations with high performers with whom you might feel a camaraderie and not engage in the same way with others who perform differently.

- Don't spend more or less time with any one group or individual based on performance.
- Don't offer, or ask for, favors of any individual or group based on performance. Give opportunities and rewards fairly.

See Chapter 9 for Optional Assignment.

Words to Know

- Incivility
- MUDA
- Feedback
- Idiosyncratic rater effect

How Much Do You Remember?

1. What percentage of employees say the feedback they receive improves their work?
   a. 75 percent
   b. 26 percent
   c. 14 percent
   d. 3 percent
2. Here are some examples of behaviors. Put a checkmark beside those which are determined actions and would require corrective action.
   - Putting the wrong taillight on
   - Arguing with a supervisor
   - Smoking in the plant
   - Being drunk or drinking on the job
   - Not wearing safety glasses when working with welding equipment
   - Being 4 minutes late for shift
   - Not doing what he or she was asked to do—this is the first time, e.g., move some steel coils from one part of the plant to another
   - Mistreating another employee, e.g., harassing a coworker
   - Using the incorrect tools
   - Taking a shortcut that will impact quality
   - Deliberately withholding information that will impact someone else negatively

- Regularly engaging in shop talk or negativity
- Stealing a piece of equipment or some supplies
- Failing to interact effectively with coworkers
- Not doing part of the job for the whole shift (missing parts or tools)

3. A communication tool that offers an opportunity for relationship building, tracking progress, and problem-solving is called:
   a. Variance
   b. Six Sigma
   c. Reliant measure
   d. Feedback

4. An SOP is:
   a. Standard Open Position
   b. Strategic Operating Plan
   c. Standing Only Procedure
   d. Standard Operating Procedure

Recommended Reading

Masotti, C. 2020. *Social Competence for Manufacturing Supervisors*. Manitoba, Canada: Propriety Publishing.

Homework Assignment

Review the workplace culture change model below and then conduct research to find another (different) model for workplace change. Write a 1,000-word essay comparing the pros and cons of the two models.

Four Key Steps—Workplace Culture Change via the Masotti Methods

Step 1: Assessment and Training—Start at Leadership Level— Fundamentals of Presence and Social Intelligence

- Assess leaders' ability to:
  - Be present and focused
  - Build trust
  - Use social intelligence
  - Consider cultural components and nuances, e.g., organizational and demographic

    ○ Convey respect in communications, e.g., when giving feedback and giving instructions

    ○ Document appropriately, e.g., end in mind, fact-based, measurable

    ○ Deliver customized training in social intelligence and civil communications, and humanity at work

Step 2: Assessment and Observation of Current Communication and Feedback Practice

    ○ Review job task lists and SOPs

    ○ Conduct periodic job observation

Step 3: Interrupt the Current Practice and Teach Masotti Behavior/Feedback Intervention Strategies

    ○ Training to include:

       ■ Asking questions (3)

       ■ Identify conscious and unconscious bias

       ■ Extend civility and courtesy, e.g., tone

       ■ Give feedback that is quantifiable, targeted, and specific

       ■ Focus on behavior versus the person

Step 4: Coach Next Level Manager to Use the Intervention

    ○ Employ coaching skills to train next level managers; do so based on experiential learning.

Advanced Thinking—Preparing for Chapter 8

Four Common Mistakes Leaders Make

In my experience, there are four common mistakes that leaders make. I believe it is critical that supervisors and managers self-identify which of these mistakes apply to them and work to avoid them prior to assessing and giving feedback to their team, and/or before engaging with employees to problem-solve.

Error #1: Failing to address their unconscious bias, e.g., having preconceived notions about what a union employee is like, his or her motivations, etc.; having a bias against women or youth or older employees without even recognizing that he or she has that bias.

Error #2: Failing to assess his or her own adaptive capacity, e.g., is he or she experiencing some change fatigue—too tired to make changes, too tied to old habits to ask questions, too prideful or ego-oriented to admit that he or she doesn't know everything.

Error #3: Failing to assume the best of others, e.g., he or she is focused—maybe due to regularity of need—on negative outcomes, what people are doing wrong, what needs to be corrected, what isn't working etc., versus focusing on what is working, and what is going right.

Error #4: Failing to ask questions, e.g., not being curious, not wondering, not asking why or how. Good leaders are not only always asking questions, they also wait for, and listen to the answers. Don't stop at one question. Make it a habit to ask a minimum of three questions in every situation.

What do you think?

CHAPTER 8

Making the Box Smaller—Reducing Variability Technique

The first rule of any technology used in business is that automation applied to an efficient operation will magnify the efficiency. The second is that automation applied to an inefficient operation will magnify the inefficiency.

—Bill Gates

A key aspect of any manufacturing leader's job is problem-solving. At the supervisory level, leaders are typically tasked with managing the people who complete the day-to-day processes and sometimes—even when civil communication is part of the process—situations will arise where a simple feedback, observation, and assessment loop doesn't adequately resolve the problem.

Still, even when situations are complex, or when it seems there is not a solution to a problem, leaders need to somehow reduce variability—that is, they need to find a way to eliminate barriers to productivity. These barriers may be real or perceived, and it doesn't matter which. The fact is, when an employee provides a reason for not performing—no matter how unreasonable that reason might be—the leader (in most cases the supervisor) has to resolve the situation.

Based on 20+ years in the field, I have come to use a method I call "making the box smaller." This approach is basically a way of removing barriers and eliminating variability. Concurrent with resolving the problem that is preventing or delaying productivity, this method serves as a training tool as well because it teaches employees that they are required to do their jobs despite barriers and that they have an obligation to report barriers as well as to work to eliminate those barriers.

The "make the box smaller" method is a combined communication and problem-solving strategy for managing employees and situations where work is not being done due to real or perceived barriers. The process helps to eliminate real or perceived barriers and helps eliminate **variability**.

This method is based on the idea that there are "levels" or "boxes" of variability. For our purposes, "variability" refers to inconsistencies, changes, or options in a typical situation or context.

Supervisors/managers have to get the job done, no matter what. So, they are continually solving problems. Some of these problems are based on variability related to legitimate concerns that an employee might have, e.g., equipment or safety issues. And, some of the problems are due to variability related to less legitimate reasons like excuses. The supervisors have to figure out how to get the work done while:

- Wasting as little time as possible
- Wasting as little resources, other than time, as possible
- Maintaining composure and control of the situation
- Supporting the employee, e.g., assuaging his or her concerns whether legitimate or not
- Setting a good example, e.g., through positive people treatment for other employees and peers who may be observing
- Meeting expectations for standards such as safety, quality, etc.

Leaders would use the "make the box smaller" method when:

- It has been identified that someone is not doing his or her job
- Checking in, e.g., observing, testing, reviewing tasks, with an employee on the job
- There is a new employee and they want to ensure he or she understands his or her job
- Giving feedback based on a negative observation, e.g., due to seeing something is wrong—maybe someone is doing his or her job but

there are issues related to efficiency or other reasons. Someone may be following the SOP, but things are not as smooth as they should be.

Before interacting with the individual/employee, leaders need:

- An up-to-date job description for the individual/employee being approached (this interaction might take place at the employee's station). NOTE: Sometimes, like for instance, when there is tension or past difficulty in communications, it's not always a good idea to show up to interact with a busy employee, clipboard or notebook in hand, as this can cause stress or mistrust.
- Appropriate documents, e.g., performance evaluation, document for recording observations, checklist, safety sheet
- IMPORTANT—Leaders are encouraged to build trust and rapport with their team on an ongoing basis and in advance of formal performance reviews. Getting in the habit of treating people well typically eliminates excuse-making and employees tend to take pride in their work and be more accountable.

Here is how the Masotti Make the Box Smaller Method works. There are five steps:

Step 1. Embed positive people treatment. This means that people are treated fairly and consistently. They are encouraged to raise concerns and when they do so, supervisors listen with the intent to understand and to support. HOW supervisors talk and act—their tone of voice, their nonverbal cues, their words all matter and should be carefully considered. When this happens, there is increased TRUST. Over time, the Civility Experts Inc. team has learned that an estimated 50 percent of the "barriers" or issues in the biggest box of issues and variability preventing or slowing performance relates to lack of trust. Some examples of issues that fall into this category might include:
    - Employee being upset because a supervisor said he would do something and did not do it

- Promises related to scheduling, breaks, or personal needs were not met or followed through on
- Employee feels disrespected or mistreated in some way, e.g., spoken to rudely, ignored, harsh public criticism by supervisor
- Employee does not feel like his or her supervisor or the company care about him or her, e.g., issues with safety or equipment or personal protection equipment, etc.
- Employee legitimately has cause not to trust, e.g., history of bullying or bias or mistreatment
- Employee does not feel supported, e.g., needs training or help and may have asked for it previously but was not heard
- Employee is not psychologically safe, e.g., threat of layoff or plant closure, etc.
- Employee has personality conflict with another employee

To reduce variability in this box which is the largest and holds the most common issues/variability, supervisors should be especially careful to watch for nonverbal and visual cues that might indicate:

- Disappointment
- Disengagement
- Anger
- Mental distress
- Exhaustion
- Physical illness
- Emotional stress
  Supervisors can ask questions such as:
- How are you feeling today?
- Is there anything that would make your job easier?
- You don't seem as effective on the job today—is there anything we can do to support you?
- Are you well enough to work?
- What specifically is prohibiting you from doing your job?
  Note: You want to be as specific as possible with the questions you ask and how you respond. The point is people

think they are doing their job and when they don't, they believe they have legitimate reasons for not doing it. So you need to be able to counter the "reasons" (many of which are actually not valid and would be labeled from a supervisory point of view as excuses).

Step 2. Set clear expectations. This means that the supervisor clearly describes and details the expectations of the job—the schedule, the policies, the job tasks, standards to be met, etc. When this information is successfully relayed, this builds ALIGNMENT, meaning the employee knows his or her job and how he or she fits in and contributes to the team. He or she knows what is being measured and what the goals are. Field research suggests that about 25 percent of barriers/issues are held in this "box" and can be addressed with the right questions.

Issues raised by employees that fit in this box frequently relate to:
- Unclear expectations
- Misinformation, e.g., outdated job description
- Supplies, e.g., not enough or incorrect items
- Equipment, e.g., maintenance issues
- Training, e.g., skills gaps
- Mixed messages, e.g., different directives from different supervisors
- Safety or injury, e.g., issues that are in process or have happened already

Step 3. Observe and document. This includes performance reviews, daily SOP and job description reviews, job task observations, and data gathering. When these activities are done consistently and in a timely way, the outcome is ACCOUNTABILITY. When performance expectations are set and measured, there is less room for variability. Field research suggests that about 15 percent of variability issues fall into this box. Issues that might be raised by employees would include:
- How come 40 units was enough yesterday and today you want 45?
- That's not what my job description says.

     ○ I can't do that task that way due to X.

     ○ If X in Y department would do his job, I could do mine.

     ○ Since when is quality more important than quantity?

In this box, the supervisor is going to ask questions related to the job tasks, but ask them in a specific way. For example, "Here are 14 lines of your job task. You acknowledged you know them, you can do them, you have what you need to do your job, is this correct?" Basically, the employee has told you he or she can do his or her job instead of you telling the employee that he or she can't do it.

CIVILITY AS CONTINUOUS IMPROVEMENT MODEL©

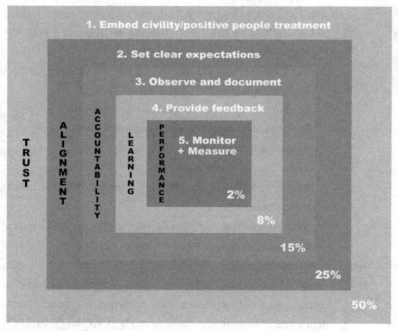

*Figure 16 Civility as Continuous Improvement Model© Masotti &
Bayer 2020*

Positive observation during the "make the box smaller" approach

Following my method of giving feedback, to encourage trust and to build relationships with people, you need to start with observations of your own. When you see something positive in a person or in their performance, mention it to the individual. State that you saw them do something good, or that they have improved on a metric. State what the improvement or good behavior is. Then tell them what the improvement or behavior means for them, for you as a supervisor or manager, and for the people around them or the company. Then tell them what you would like to see in the future. The future statement could be to encourage them to share other ideas about their own job or the jobs of others. This feedback process will encourage a collaborative culture.

NOTE: The supervisor should be documenting all these conversations.

Negative observation during the "make the box smaller" approach

Negative observations need to be treated in a timely manner as well. Using the same procedure, mention the negative quantitative, qualitative observation or behavior. Let the person know how the observation affects the individual, you, their metrics, and the people around them. To correct the negative results or behavior let the person know what you expect in the future.

Quantitative or qualitative observations of your own encourage feedback from employees and help to improve a process or condition.

To correct a toxic culture and to make a culture of continuous improvement, a pattern of feedback is needed from you. Give positive and negative feedback on a daily basis. Do not wait for scenarios like a performance review at the end of the year to highlight good or negative feedback. Does it make sense to outline poor performance or good performance on events that possibly occurred months or almost a year ago? It would be better to give daily feedback to expedite results and to put a plan in place daily rather than wait weeks or months to address issues.

Step 4. Provide feedback. This step includes interacting and communicating with a strategic and specific purpose—either to give positive or negative feedback. The Masotti Feedback Method is recommended (see Chapter 7). Field research shows that about 8 percent of issues/variability fall into this box. When feedback is effective, the outcome is LEARNING.

Issues/variability that might be expressed by employees if you get to this box usually relate to:

o Change in directive that was not conveyed at all to the employee

o Varying directives, e.g., day supervisor versus night supervisor

o Feedback had not been provided at all

Step 5. Monitor and measure. In this step, the cycle continues. In addition to observation and feedback, facts and real data are collected and documented. These metrics are used to evaluate behavior and performance change as well as the overall impact of the performance on the organization. Field research shows that about 2 percent of variability fits into this box. When behavior is monitored and measured, one of the outcomes is higher performance. Issues raised by employees in this box typically relate to:

o I have not had a performance review in X months/years, etc.

o No one told me the goals have changed.

o I am invisible here, so I just keep doing what I do.

Once you resolve the issues and reduce variability in whichever "box" the employee is in, an effective closing strategy is to say, "You need to let me know when you can't do your job." This statement or requirement offsets many excuses because it obligates an employee to be accountable. There is no way out of this directive. The box is very small, there is very little room to move, and there is only one way to resolve the issue when you get to this point. Basically, the employee cannot stop working for any reason UNLESS he or she first lets the supervisor know there is an issue, versus the typical behavior which is for most employees to stop working based on their perception of variability and then make the supervisor aware.

Over time, using this method builds trust because you are not criticizing, blaming, embarrassing, or parenting an adult employee. You are just supervising in that you are working to resolve problems and make the employee's job easier. If you stick to facts and questions, make statements versus give opinions, focus on actions versus emotions, the result is task-orientation and process communications. This type of interaction does not come across as personal. This is important for building credibility plus this method is an approach that even new or inexperienced supervisors can apply consistently. Even if you don't know anything about the jobs the employees are doing, you ask specific questions that require specific responses.

If you pay attention and listen to the employee's responses, you will learn, and at the same time, you are putting accountability onto the operator/employee, and you are giving him or her the power to manage the interaction. This locus of control is a critical balancing act if you want to build trust in workplaces.

If when you approach the employee you are met with high resistance, shop talk, assertive behavior, swearing, etc., avoid responding in kind. Instead focus on the document and the requirements of the job. You are in a way applying corrective actions for every excuse…BUT, while you are addressing the excuses, you are doing so in a civil way. Your body language doesn't show frustration or exasperation, and you aren't name-calling or engaging in shop talk.

This way, employees cannot comment on how you delivered the information. Your communication style cannot become a point of variability (would be in Box 1). Instead, the emphasis is on the workplace document and details in the instructions. This tones things down—it's not about personality or emotion.

For Consideration—Making the Box Smaller

Review the key questions and possible employee responses below. Then write how you would respond to "make the box smaller" if you were a supervisor.

Key Questions to Ask to Initiate Interaction

A) Hello X, just noticed (or Y mentioned), that you are not doing Z. Can you tell me why you are not doing Z?

B) Hi X, wanted to check in and see how things are going. Let's take a few minutes and run through your job description…

C) X, we have changed/updated your job description so I want to ensure that you can do Z.

Possible Responses Include:

1. I don't have time to do Z.

   Recommended response:

2. I don't know how to do Z.

   Recommended response:

3. I wasn't trained to do Z.

   Recommended response:

4. Boss A told me to do Y instead of Z.

   Recommended response:

5. It's not my job to do Z.

   Recommended response:

6. I can't do Z due to an injury.

   Recommended response:

7. I don't have permission to do Z.

   Recommended response:

8. I don't have the right tools to do Z.

   Recommended response:

9. If I do Z, then X will happen.

   Recommended response:

10. I would do Z except I don't want to help Y.

    Recommended response:

11. If I help Y, I can't get my own work done.

    Recommended response:

12. This is a new upgrade.

    Recommended response:

13. I know what to do but I'm not doing it.

    Recommended response:

14. It's not safe to do what you are asking.

    Recommended response:

For Review

At the end of Chapter 7, in the Advanced Thinking section, I mentioned four mistakes that leaders often make. They are listed below.

Four Common Mistakes Leaders Make

In my experience, there are four common mistakes that leaders make. I believe it is critical that supervisors and managers self-identify which of these mistakes apply to them and work to avoid them prior to assessing and giving feedback to their team, and/or before engaging with employees to problem-solve.

Error #1: Failing to address their unconscious bias, e.g., having preconceived notions about what a union employee is like, his or her motivations, etc.; having a bias against women or youth or older employees without even recognizing that he or she has that bias.

Error #2: Failing to assess his or her own adaptive capacity, e.g., is he or she experiencing some change fatigue—too tired to make changes, too tied to old habits to ask questions, too prideful or ego-oriented to admit that he or she doesn't know everything.

Error #3: Failing to assume the best of others, e.g., he or she is focused—maybe due to regularity of need—on negative outcomes, what people are doing wrong, what needs to be corrected, what isn't working etc., versus focusing on what is working, what is going right.

Error #4: Failing to ask questions, e.g., not being curious, not wondering, not asking why or how. Good leaders are not only always asking questions, they also wait for, and listen to the answers. Don't stop at one question. Make it a habit to ask a minimum of three questions in every situation.

After reviewing the "make the box smaller" approach, it should be clear that these are mistakes that need to be avoided in order to be an effective problem-solver.

Some additional considerations include:

1. Wait until the individual is coming back from a break, i.e., extend their break.
2. Make sure someone suitable can cover the person while you are interacting with them.
3. Make sure you are speaking in private.
4. Ensure you smile as you approach the individual so that he or she does not assume he or she is in trouble or that there is a problem.
5. Try to keep the interaction to 10 to 15 minutes.
6. Stick to the issue at hand, e.g., don't get into social chit chat—ensure the individual recognizes that the feedback is the important piece of the communication.

Nonverbal tips:

• Avoid leaning forward, which can be interpreted as aggressive.

Verbal tips:

• Remember that the employee suspects or expects that this is a first step to discipline. This makes the interaction stressful for both parties. Let the employee know that this is not necessarily the case.
• Try to diffuse or allay any fear or assumptions the employee might have.
• Try to put people at ease. Smile, say hello, make eye contact. They need to get used to having interactions with you that are non-threatening. This is why building rapport and trust on an ongoing basis is critical. You don't need to be personal, but you do need to interact about positive things, work-related outcomes, people's vacation schedules, a company event, some achievement, or something positive, maybe company news.

- When building rapport, you have to ask questions about things you can honestly and legitimately show interest in. For example, if you don't care what someone did on the weekend, don't ask that question. Ask questions about experience on the job, past work, workplace goals, e.g., say something like, "Wow, you've been here 20 years, you must know a lot about this place." (Makes the person feel good and also acknowledges his or her experience.)
- Avoid adding in "I" statements—don't inject your own experiences or stories into the conversation. Keep the focus on the other person.

Remember, you cannot control the other person. But you can change your own behavior. You can control what you do in response to someone else. You can't control how they will react, or what is going on in their home. You need to be ready for when it does happen; you need to have a plan—don't just let it blow up in your face because it's going to happen. Upset happens, irate happens. Screaming and yelling happens. When these things happen and people seem out of control, give people an out—don't corner them, don't set them up…don't back them up and force defensiveness. You can do the following:

- Offer a break.
- Don't just list what they do wrong.
- Give them an opportunity to say what they need or want.
- Let them make a decision.
- Offer options—ask if they have ideas.
- Don't tell them what to do directly—they need to know the job.
- Talk facts, not persona. Remain calm even if they are not, as they will reflect on how you reacted.
- Maintain your power—don't give up.

See Chapter 9 for Optional Assignment.

Words to Know
- Variability

How Much Do You Remember?

1. "Variability" is…
   a. inconsistencies, changes, or options in a typical situation or context
   b. the way things change in a geographical area
   c. how people adapt to change
   d. the degree to which change can be managed
2. Step 2 in the "make the box smaller" method is…
   a. embed civility
   b. observe
   c. set expectations
   d. monitor and measure
   e. provide feedback
3. To change workplace culture, it is a good idea to give feedback how often?
   a. Once a week
   b. Once a year
   c. Once a day
   d. Once a month
4. Civility Experts Inc. field research shows that what percentage of variability related to solving people problems falls in the outside/largest "box" and is related to trust?
   a. 15 percent
   b. 8 percent
   c. 75 percent
   d. 50 percent

Recommended Reading

Whitepaper. "Factory of the Future." www.anixter.com/content/dam/Suppliers/Hitachi/iecWP-futurefactory-LR-en.pdf. Published 2015, 08/31/2020

Homework Assignment

There are five commonly used approaches to problem-solving. Research them (below) and write a 2,000-word essay describing each of them. Be sure to include details about when each approach would be most useful when applied to manufacturing.

1. Five "WHYs" technique
2. PROACT technique
3. CREATIVE technique
4. COLLABORATIVE technique
5. PLAN, DO, CHECK, ACT technique

Advanced Thinking—Preparing to Use What You Have Learned

Take some time to review all eight chapters and write a list of the top 10 concepts, definitions, facts, or strategies that you have learned that you can apply to your current work or life.

CHAPTER 9

Putting It All Together

It is not the employer who pays the wages. He only handles the money.
It is the product that pays the wages.

—Henry Ford, 1922

Snapshot Takeaway

To build a culture of civility in manufacturing workplaces, you would do
the following:

1. **Implement Prong/Step #1 of the Trident Approach**
   Step 1—Part A: Assessment and Training—Start at Leadership
   Level—Fundamentals of Presence and Social Intelligence
   - Assess leaders' ability to:
   - Be present and focused
   - Build trust
   - Use social intelligence
   - Consider cultural components and nuances, e.g., organizational and demographic
   - Convey respect in communications, e.g., when giving feedback and giving instructions
   - Document appropriately, e.g., end in mind, fact-based, measurable
   - Use tools like the culture Indicator continuum to assess leaders' state, in terms of overall current civility.
   - Deliver customized training in social intelligence and civil communications, and humanity-at-work training to the top levels.

Step 1—Part B:

- ○ Assess the work teams, e.g., by individual skills assessment, the civility symptoms survey, the civility culture compass, the culture indicator continuum, etc. to identify skills gaps.
- ○ Deliver adapted versions of the social intelligence training, civil communication training, and/or customized civility training (e.g., building trust) to all other levels of employees. Or, if budget is an issue, devise a plan including roll out, learning objectives, and evaluation strategies whereby the upper levels and leaders teach and coach their teams to be civil by leading with civility. (This has to be structured, required, and measured. For example, you can't just say, "Go lead your teams.")

2. **Implement Prong/Step #2 of the Trident Approach**
   Assessment and Observation of Current Communication and Feedback Practice for Aspects of Civility
   - Review job task lists and SOPs
   - Conduct periodic job observation
   - Assess overall workplace:
     - ○ Trust (a good indicator of engagement)
     - ○ Morale
     - ○ Wellness, e.g., deeper than morale and includes resilience and hardiness
     - ○ Continuous learning skills
     - ○ Systems thinking skills
     - ○ Cultural competence skills
     - ○ General metrics, e.g.,
       - ▪ Absenteeism
       - ▪ Error rates
       - ▪ Quality

   And, where causal factors for poor assessment outcomes are symptoms of incivility, apply the civility–incivility filter.

3. **Implement Prong/Step #3 of the Trident Approach**
   Interrupt the Current Practice and Teach Masotti Behavior/Feedback Intervention Strategies
   - Training to include:
     - ○ Asking questions (3)

- ○ Identify conscious and unconscious bias
- ○ Extend civility and courtesy, e.g., tone
- ○ Give feedback that is quantifiable, targeted, and specific
- ○ Focus on behavior versus the person

4. **Continue the process: Coach next-level manager to use the intervention**

- Employ coaching skills to train next-level managers and build their civility competencies. Do so based on experiential learning and on-the-job training.

Answer Key

Chapter 1—For Consideration: Forecasted Trends and Influences 1

In reviewing the three significant events that changed manufacturing, how would you describe how these events impacted **workplace culture** in manufacturing organizations?

Topic 1: Industry 4.0 Comes of Age

How do you think this trend (robotics and the "Internet of Things" in manufacturing) will impact workplace culture in manufacturing organizations?

Possible Response

- People need to learn new skills, e.g., how to operate the robots.
- People might initially be afraid of the changes, or that they would lose their jobs.
- There would be potentially fewer jobs, or different jobs and potentially higher paying jobs for those who operate the robotics.
- It would potentially make costs of manufacturing higher initially, e.g., investments in robotics, and then potentially higher profits.
- There would be potentially higher efficiency.

---

[1]Manufacturing Global. 2018. "Manufacturing Sector Set for Significant Change in 2018." www.manufacturingglobal.com/logistics/manufacturing-sector-set-significant -change-2018. 06/08/2019

All of these things might impact culture in that people might be fear-ful or have low trust or resist change and new learning. In addition, there could be potential fear related to shift time change, duration of shifts, number of persons on shifts, etc.

Topic 2: *Customer Experience Is King*

What types of new processes do you think will have to be implemented to help manage the people side of these new high-tech systems?

Possible Response

- Potentially more on-demand work—so training and shift change processes
- Processes to monitor and train production teams' ability to deliver aspects of customer service
- Potentially different systems in sales and marketing to assess and evaluate customer needs
- Potentially more transparency in terms of how things are manufac-tured, e.g., sources and ingredients, suppliers, social impact, envi-ronmental impact, etc., so, processes to track and document and report all of these aspects
- Potentially more customization and so processes to enable special orders and custom elements, e.g., product details, inventory, costs, suppliers, quotes, equipment required, etc.
- Potentially need to incorporate processes to assess and evaluate costs and manpower related to delivering custom orders
- Potentially need to build teams' ability to collaborate and commu-nicate to work together to meet service expectations
- Potentially a process for sharing information with the team in ad-vance of the surprise/change, etc.

Topic 3: *AI-Driven Future*

Given that many manufacturing organizations have large numbers of long-term employees who are sometimes resistant to change, what plan would you put in place to try to offset the potential fear, lack of change readiness, and general resistance to AI in the workplace?

Possible Response

- Share the benefit of the change to the individual employees—be honest.
- Give the details and information to the front-line, long-term employees, being as transparent as possible. Try to avoid surprises. For example, give the timeline, etc.
- Where possible, implement pre-training or raise awareness.
- Check in to see that the employees are adapting/adjusting.

Optional Assignment (Answers Will Vary; Discuss with Your Trainer and/or the Training Group)

Review the chart below and choose one of the trends listed. Write a 1,500-word essay detailing your findings about the specifics of this trend including:

- Causal factors
- Impact to employees
- Impact to employer
- Recommendations for mitigating impact

Civility Experts Inc. international team suggests that the following are the top issues/challenges facing manufacturing organizations as we head towards 2025 and into the next decade:

- Lack of skilled labor, e.g., there is a growing manufacturing skills gap
- Challenges due to a multi-generational workforce; specifically, attracting and retaining employees and meeting expectations for employee satisfaction

- Lack of "culture for quality" i.e., quality standards issues; specifically, a need to eliminate closed-loop quality management, e.g., problems being solved within silos but not shared/applied to larger organization
- Balancing project deadlines while still producing quality products; specifically, providing advanced project management and managing lower costs and rising quality, especially related to international/overseas suppliers
- Need for better supply-chain visibility/production workflow to improve performance and reduce costs (competitive pricing/increase revenue growth)
- Ability to effectively measure quality metrics/performance indicators; specifically, maximizing technological intelligence/data mining and ensuring readiness to handle exponential data growth
- Poor customer service, for example, related to self-service trends (use of technology), which results in a need to be customer-adaptive
- Difficulties integrating old with new technologies while maintaining/improving quality and efficiencies, e.g., cybersecurity
- Time loss due to regional and national compliance requirements
- Maintaining and monitoring safety mindset amidst increasing automation

Chapter 1—For Review

a) What are the possible benefits of a command and control management style?

Possible Response(s)

- You don't have to train people to think, they just do what they're told.
- You don't need to build trust because you rule and lead by fear; people don't ask questions.
- You can have supervisors and managers who are promoted from the floor with high technical skills, but no people skills and they are potentially still successful at meeting goals.

b) Why do you think command and control management style was/is prevalent in many manufacturing organizations?

Possible Response(s)

- Historically, during depression and hard times, people were just happy to have a job, so they did whatever they had to in order to keep it.
- In the past, people with no education or experience could work in manufacturing and learn on the job, and maybe they didn't have a lot of other opportunities.
- The mentality was that production employees were lower in level in terms of what they had to offer, e.g., people knew and accepted their place.
- Manufacturing companies were owned by very rich families who behaved how they wished and could sometimes take advantage of wealth and influence, e.g., were not held accountable for poor people treatment.

c) What trends and influences might prompt organizations to move away from a power-focused management style?

Possible Response(s)

- Powerful unions holding management accountable for how people are treated
- Individuals with more access to, and understanding of, their rights
- Individual expectations for opportunities and growth, e.g., training, promotion, etc.
- Organizations implementing different management styles are seeing faster and greater improvements concurrent with cost savings
- Continuous improvement benefits of collaborative and happy work teams, i.e., there is a business case for treating people well
- Legislation such as respectful workplace policies, anti-harassment, health, and safety regulations

Quiz Answers

1. Traditional power-focused management style in manufacturing has resulted in what kind of workplace culture?
   a. Overt controlling
   b. Commander as leader
   c. **Command and control**
   d. None of the above
2. Team knowledge is:
   a. information specific to the first manufacturing companies ever created
   b. knowledge about processes that only the employees know
   c. **knowledge learning on the job that isn't known to everyone**
   d. a and b
3. Traditional power-focused manufacturing workplace culture can create levels of trust sufficient such that the silo team shares information and "on the job" information that can be used appropriately because competence is assumed within the silo team. **True** or False?
4. Provide two examples of pivotal changes or events in history that impacted manufacturing.
   Industrial revolution, steam engine, mass production, automation and the information age

General Interest

Supplemental Stats and Facts[2]—For Canadian Audiences (Because the Authors Are Canadian)

1. Auto manufacturing regularly contributes over $20 billion to Canada's GDP.
2. Nationally, auto and parts production accounts for about 16.8 percent of manufacturing sales.

---

[2]Canada's Manufacturing Sector. 2020. "Canadian Manufacturing Sector Gateway," *Innovation, Science and Economic Development Canada.* https://www.ic.gc.ca/eic/site/mfg-fab.nsf/eng/home (Modified March 12, 2020).

3. In Ontario, transportation equipment manufacturing is 20.2 percent of GDP.
4. Direct industry employment in Canada accounts for 130,000.
5. Manufacturing is a cornerstone of our modern economy. Accounting for approximately $174 billion of our GDP, manufacturing represents more than 10 percent of Canada's total GDP. What is more, manufacturers export more than $354 billion each year, representing 68 percent of all of Canada's merchandise exports.

   All of this adds up to 1.7 million quality full-time, well-paying jobs—all across the country. And as the sector has modernized, manufacturers have become innovative and high-tech, relying on a highly skilled and knowledgeable workforce that includes designers, researchers, programmers, engineers, technicians, and tradespeople.

   Canada's manufacturing industry has huge potential for its economic future. The world is changing, and new technologies are not just opening new markets for Canadian goods, they are changing the ways these goods are produced. For manufacturing in Canada to remain a vibrant, innovative, and competitive contributor to our economy, business, and government will need to work together. A vibrant manufacturing community encourages industrial clusters that develop skills, knowledge, and technology. Success breeds success: when Canada's manufacturers grow and compete, they act as magnets for new investment and for new young people wanting to be part of this great industry, making the products of tomorrow.
6. In 2017, the Canadian economy had the following relative weighting by industry, as percentage value of GDP:

Canada is one of the few developed nations that is a net exporter of energy—in 2009, net exports of energy products amounted to 2.9 percent of the GDP. Most important are the large oil and gas resources centered in Alberta and the Northern Territories, but also present in neighboring British Columbia and Saskatchewan. The vast Athabasca oil sands give Canada the world's third largest reserves of oil after Saudi Arabia and Venezuela according to USGS.

Industry	Share of GDP (%)
Real estate and rental and leasing	13.01
Manufacturing	10.37
Mining, quarrying, and oil and gas extraction	8.21
Finance and insurance	7.07
Construction	7.07
Health care and social assistance	6.63
Public administration	6.28
Wholesale trade	5.78
Retail trade	5.60
Professional, scientific, and technical services	5.54
Educational services	5.21
Transportation and warehousing	4.60
Information and cultural industries	3.00
Administrative and support, waste management, and remediation services	2.46
Utilities	2.21
Accommodation and food services	2.15
Other services (except public administration)	1.89
Agriculture, forestry, fishing, and hunting	1.53
Arts, entertainment, and recreation	0.77
Management of companies and enterprises	0.62

Figure 17 Canadian GDP Chart, 2020

Chapter 2—For Consideration: Data Logistics and Real-Time Data

Question

a) What specific aspects of leadership (supervisor/manager) behavior do you think can impact an employee's experience such that an employee will trust that leader?

Possible Response(s)

- Tell the truth.
- Be behavior

- Treat all employees the same.
- Make reasonable requests.
- Always consider the employees safety—physical, psychological etc.
- Focus on competence and behavior versus personality and personal qualities.
- Reward and acknowledge at least as often as you criticize.
- Ask questions and listen to the answers.
- Don't make assumptions.
- Don't engage in shop talk.
- Speak kindly, e.g., treat people like adults, don't diminish others, acknowledge others, say thank you.
- Use people's proper names, e.g., avoid nicknames and labels.

b) How and why do you think high levels of trust might support the needs of "knowledge workers"?

Possible Response(s)

- Knowledge workers need to know that their supervisor trusts them to make some lower-level decisions.
- Knowledge workers need to be able to trust their supervisors to react and respond in reasonable ways.
- Trust fosters confidence—knowledge workers will take responsibility for their own learning if they feel trusted.

c) How would building trust and having a team of "knowledge workers" be important relative to data logistics and real-time data?

Possible Response(s)

- Managers/supervisors can't always get all the information they need, how they need it, when they need it—but if there is high trust, team members will help gather the data.
- Data is likely more consistent and accurate when there is mutual trust, e.g., less sabotage.

Optional Assignment (Answers Will Vary; Discuss with Your Trainer and/or the Training Group)

A) List at least three indicators of incivility in a workplace, e.g., how might employees behave.
B) Give two reasons employees might be dissatisfied at work, causing them to disengage.
C) How do you personally define civility? (Ensure that your definition is quantifiable.)

For Review

If you are employed, take the Civility Culture Compass Assessment© at www.civilityexperts.com and consider your results. If you are not employed, ask someone you know to take the assessment (no fee to do so) and review his or her results.

This assessment helps identify the current situation in your workplace relative to four cultural aspects that have been proven to predict successful outcomes for civility training. You receive a score from 1 to 60 in each of four compass categories. A low score (29 or lower) in any category means

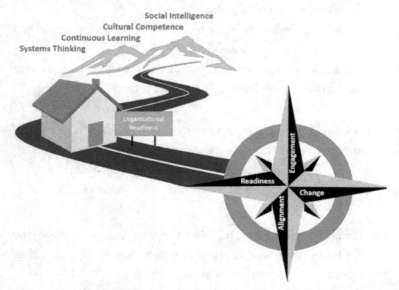

Figure 18 Civility Culture Compass Assessment© Civility Experts Inc. 2015

that you have low need for adjustment/preparation—that is, your workplace culture is satisfactory in that compass category and the likelihood that civility training will be successful is increased.

Quiz Answers

1. Stress at work accounts for what percentage of overall life stress (according to *Quality of Life* report)?
   a. 10 percent
   b. 40 percent
   c. **73 percent**
   d. 67 percent
2. Gallup *State of the American Workplace* report found that what percentage of employees in manufacturing environments are disengaged?
   a. **75 percent**
   b. 25 percent
   c. 39 percent
   d. 72 percent
3. The term for literally dropping dead at work is:
   a. katsume
   b. **karoshi**
   c. burnout
   d. disintegration
4. A knowledge worker is:
   a. an employee who may know how to do aspects of many jobs
   b. employees who are continuous learners
   c. employees who take responsibility for their own learning
   d. **all of the above**

Chapter 3—For Consideration: The Civility Indicator Iceberg

Question

Using the iceberg metaphor, draw an iceberg showing what might be below the surface for each of the following behaviors which would be observed in a manufacturing environment.

Scenario 1

Decision-making—Observed above the surface:

- Silence
- Eye-rolling
- Shrugging shoulders
- Disengagement
- Avoidance of making decisions

Possible Response(s)

- Mistrust of employer or whomever is asking for a decision
- Doesn't feel competent to make a solution
- Personality issues, e.g., doesn't like the other person
- Contempt, e.g., doesn't believe the asker really wants the answer, as nothing will be implemented anyway
- Past experience, e.g., ignored, embarrassed, humiliated
- Stressed or time-pressured, e.g., not interested, too busy, etc.

Scenario 2

Errors—Observed above the surface:

- Employee appears to have correct equipment.
- Employee appears to know what to do.
- Employee continually makes unacceptable errors.

Possible Response(s)

- Employee/operator is not trained properly.
- Employee is afraid to say he or she doesn't know the job.
- Employee is seeking attention.
- The process or procedure is being followed but isn't correct.
- Goals and expectations were not outlined.
- Errors were not tracked or documented so continued.
- Employee is deliberately sabotaging to punish supervisor/manager.

- Employee wasn't aware of impact of errors, e.g., key elements are not highlighted.
- Process was changed but hasn't been audited recently.

Scenario 3

Failure to wear safety equipment (personal protection equipment)—Observed on the surface:

- Requirements are in the employee handbook.
- Other employees on the team are wearing PPE.
- Supervisor has asked employee to put PPE on.
- Employee has been provided with the equipment.

Possible Response(s)

- The equipment is broken or doesn't fit.
- There is a personal, health reason for not wearing it.
- There is anger about another issue, e.g., management isn't following the rules (wearing PPE, paying fairly, giving holiday).
- Employee has requested a new piece of equipment and/or a replacement, or a repair on other safety element. Possible response would be, "I asked you to fix the guard nine weeks ago and you are suddenly concerned about my safety glasses."
- No consistency across managers/supervisors and enforcement, e.g., one shift lead requires it, one does not.
- No follow through or accountability, e.g., if people continue to break the rules and there is no discipline.

Optional Assignment (Answers Will Vary; Discuss with Your Trainer and/or the Training Group)

Optional Assignment

The American Management Association commissioned the Human Resource Institute to conduct a global, in-depth study on strategic agility and resilience. The Institute's series of "Major Issues" surveys showed that "managing

change" was perennially ranked among the top workforce management issues throughout the 1990s and into this past decade and through to 2030.

Some of the main findings were:

- The vast majority of respondents (82 percent) report that the pace
  of change experienced by their organizations has increased compared with 5 years ago.
- A majority (69 percent) say that their organizations had experienced disruptive change—that is, severe surprises or unanticipated
  shocks—over the previous 12 months.
- There are meaningful differences among surveyed organizations
  in the highest- and lowest-performing categories. Compared with
  their lower-performing counterparts, higher performers were more
  likely to:
  - View themselves as agile and resistant
  - See change as an opportunity
  - Say that the pace of change has gotten faster but remains
    predictable
  - View themselves as having better change capacities at the indi-
    vidual, team, and organizational levels
  - Engage in strategies such as training to improve managers'
    change-management skills

Additionally, the Conference Board of Canada found that CEOs
around the globe identify "speed, flexibility, and adaptability to change"
as among their greatest concerns. "Adapt or die" seems to be a prevail-
ing attitude. Accordingly, companies of the future will benefit by finding
good ways of measuring their capacity to manage change—that is, their
"adaptive capacity."[3] These organizations will be able to gauge their current agility and resilience and then determine additional needs. When
gauging adaptive capacity, organizations will look at four different levels:

- The individual employee
- The team

---

[3]American Management Association. 2006–2010. "A Global Study of Current Trends
and Human Possibilities."

- The organization
- The industry[4]

Write a 1,500-word essay describing what skills you think employees need in order to be change-ready. Be able to rationalize your viewpoint and don't forget to provide sources and resources.

Quiz Answers

1. According to Gallup, what percentage of change initiatives fail?
   a. 35 percent
   b. 62 percent
   c. **70 percent**
   d. 90 percent
2. The iceberg theory is sometimes called what?
   a. The theory of everything
   b. **The theory of omission**
   c. Hemmingway method
   d. Surface theory
3. According to Masotti & Bayer, workplace culture is "the habits, traditions, attitudes, tone of interactions, and general behaviors that make up employees' day-to-day experience." **True** or False?
4. In order of application, the three prongs in the Masotti Trident Approach are:
   a. Assessment, training, feedback
   b. Evaluation, training, feedback
   c. **Training, assessment, feedback**
   d. Feedback, assessment, training

QUESTION: Based on what you now understand to be incivility, what types of "events" (perceived issues, challenges, crisis, problems) that might be assigned as continuous improvement projects—what we can call "low-hanging fruit" could be resolved easily through civility, e.g., never get to the point where they are identified as "events"?

---

[4]The Conference Board. 2005.https://cmcoutperform.com/sites/default/files/Agility-andResilienceGlobalStudy.pdf 05/05/2019

Chapter 4—For Consideration:
The Civility in Practice Model

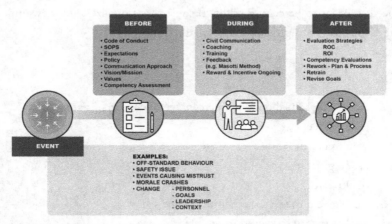

Figure 19 Civility in Practice Model©, Masotti & Bayer 2018

Possible Response(s)

- Employees not following day-to-day processes and rules; when it is identified that the reason they are not following the rules is tied to resentment or mistrust, avoidance, or sabotage, this is about civility.
- Employees are not engaging in required socialization activities, e.g., signing up for team softball, golf tournaments, book club, holiday charity events, etc.

These "issues" can all be resolved through building relational skills. These are not problems that continuous improvement resources should be spent on.

QUESTION: Why do you think some supervisors and/or employees would opt NOT to engage in civility best practices in spite of knowing the benefits?

Possible Response(s)

- Some people like to create drama so that they can be the hero and resolve it.

- Some people are just not comfortable with change and even positive things like engaging in civility require a person to change.
- Some people like to keep the power imbalanced, e.g., they like to have emotional or physical power and control over others.
- Some people have backgrounds or religious beliefs that justify them behaving in what might be perceived as uncivil to others but seems natural or okay to them, e.g., treating women differently than men.
- Some people truly have not experienced civility and so they do not recognize the values of it, i.e., they are accustomed to angry voices or humiliation etc., and so they see it as normal.

QUESTION: We know from the research that civility at work can increase innovation, retention, trust, and collaboration. What other, more personal or individual impacts can you perceive if civility becomes part of the employees' day-to-day experience?

Possible Response(s)

Research also shows that civility at work can reduce stress and when we reduce stress we can improve how people react to situations, e.g., driving; we can impact their relationships, e.g., they don't take the stress home; and we can impact their overall health, e.g., potentially avoid the need for avoidant behaviors or alcohol abuse, etc., as ways of managing stress at work.

QUESTION: What is the risk if civility best practices are not exhibited continuously, that is, before, during, and after an "event"?

Possible Response(s)

- Repairs happen too late or don't happen at all.
- When behavior isn't consistent, people don't always trust the reason for the behavior when it does happen.
- When civility isn't consistent, people may not immediately associate the positive behavior as causal, e.g., tie it to a positive outcome.
- Civility is less likely to become ingrained in workplace culture if it is not exhibited on an ongoing basis and across the organization.

Optional Assignment #1 (Answers Will Vary; Discuss with Your Trainer and/or the Training Group)

Consider an international turbomachinery manufacturer. In keeping with their culture of continuous improvement, the organization is seeking a new approach to training that can address bottom line business metrics related to key performance indicators, build team engagement, and improve workplace culture overall. As such, the organization has identified that they have good data and good methods/tools, but it is the people element that needs business excellence support.

In addition, there is good awareness of culture and performance issues as well as engagement at higher levels; however, there are perceived to be some engagement challenges where the focus seems to be on quick wins to deliver against targets. Team communication, collaboration, alignment, service, and performance are suffering as a result.

What would you do? What questions would you ask? How would you solve this problem and what specific solutions would you offer in order to do the following?

- Gather bottom line business metrics in a meaningful way.
- Track and/or improve key performance indicators.
- Build team engagement.
- Improve workplace culture.

Optional Assignment #2 (Answers Will Vary; Discuss with Your Trainer and/or the Training Group)

Applying the Continuum—Practice Activity

1. A supervisor is known for being indirect when interacting with his or her team. Due to a lack of clarity, employees are not always meeting expectations and then issues arise, e.g., the supervisor has to resolve the situation, the employees are angry, etc.

   a. What behaviors might employees exhibit in this scenario to indicate that they are unhappy?

b. Based on the behaviors you might observe, listed as responses for a) above, what stage of the continuum might you place the employees on?

c. Based on your response to b) what behaviors or conditions did the supervisor contribute to create this situation?

d. What are the impacts if the supervisor does not accurately assess the situation?

e. Based on what you know about civility, if you were the supervisor, how would you resolve this situation?

Quiz Answers

1. Companies that openly promote civil communication among employees earn how much more revenue than competitors?
   a. 22 percent
   b. 87 percent
   c. 55 percent
   d. **30 percent**

2. When embedded into workplace training, policy, procedures, and best practices, civility is:
   a. retroactive
   b. reactive
   c. protractive
   d. **proactive**

3. In the civility in practice model, "ROI" refers to:
   a. regularly observed incident
   b. return on currency
   c. recommended occupation indicator
   d. **return on character**

4. Calling someone names, accusing, and deflecting are behaviors that suggest an employee is at what state on the culture indicator continuum?
   a. **Withdrawal**
   b. Adaptation
   c. Blame
   d. Defiance

Chapter 5—For Consideration

QUESTION: Why do many leaders/managers/supervisors not properly leverage the skills and knowledge of their teams?

Possible Response(s)

- Old habits, e.g., related to hierarchy
- Ego, e.g., they want to keep perceived power all to themselves
- Fear, e.g., that someone will know more than they do
- Ignorance, e.g., they never asked about or researched the skills of their teams
- General stress, e.g., they just don't have time to stop and consider these things
- Situational factors, e.g., a layoff is pending, so there is no point in getting to know people; there are other priorities, personal issues between leaders and other persons, etc.

QUESTION: What can happen if leaders do not agree that every person is equally deserving of respect?

Possible Response(s)

- Biased or unfair treatment
- Bullying or harassment
- Illegal hiring or recruiting practices
- Personal issues and mistrust
- Others

QUESTION: What happens if an individual is lacking in one of the four skills required to be civility-competent?

Possible Response(s)

- Sometimes he or she can get by, e.g., rely on social IQ to get support and help from others.
- It depends on which skill is lacking, e.g., lacking cultural competence in a diverse workplace can be problematic.

- Reliance on others can be an issue, e.g., "If I have low social skills, others can take advantage of me."
- There could be mistrust due to perceived incompetency.
- Individuals can behave in uncivil ways without realizing it.
- Others

Notes on Homework

The two scenarios represent two large auto manufacturers. I worked for both of them.

- The difference between the two approaches was vastly different as far as return on improvements.
- It also provided two different cultures and approaches to improving the performance of supervisors.
- Peer pressure was huge at Company Y and people who took on the CI projects were ridiculed and commented on constantly. What should have been a positive step was looked on as opportunistic or negative and, in my opinion, most likely prevented others from attempting projects.
- At Company X, everyone had the opportunity to improve and be supported by others. They all had a common goal and worked together to help each other.
- The savings at Company X far outperformed Company Y.

Optional Assignment (Answers Will Vary; Discuss with Your Trainer and/or the Training Group)

Choose one of the Masotti communication strategies checklists and review the list from a "culturally considerate" lens. That is, think about which, if any, of the behaviors on the list:

1. Might be misunderstood by an employee with an international cultural background
2. Might be difficult for different supervisors to exhibit, e.g., does the behavior need to change if the supervisor is old or young, man or woman, less experienced or more experienced, etc.

3. Might be perceived by "old school" manufacturing employees as touchy-feely or ineffective in a traditional command and control environment

Quiz Answers

1. Social intelligence includes:
   a. Social skills, social smarts, and social savvy
   b. Social style, social knowledge, and social savvy
   c. **Social knowledge, social radar, and social style**
   d. Social radar, social skills, and social style
2. One behavior that builds trust when communicating is:
   a. Always tell the truth.
   b. Look people in the eye.
   c. Say what you mean.
   d. **All of the above.**
3. Respect means:
   a. everyone is treated equitably.
   b. **everyone is treated as valuable.**
   c. everyone is trusted.
   d. everyone is given equal opportunities.
4. In the civility value chain, what a person does (in terms of civility) is called:
   a. action-oriented civility
   b. **civility in action**
   c. civil action
   d. actionable civility

Chapter 6—For Consideration

Situation #1: Poor Performance—Specifically, Employee Is Just Not Completing the Work

On the surface, you might assume the poor performance is due to incompetence, but when you look a little deeper you observe that it is actually due to peer pressure. How would you handle this situation?

Possible Response(s)

I have experienced situations, especially in unionized environments, where people are poor performers due to peer pressure. To be fair it is mostly due to a poor culture. When determining why a person is not performing and investigating why a person is not performing, we have to ask questions if it is due to peer pressure. Sometimes people will perform at their minimum level because they do not want to stand out from the rest of the group. To combat this situation, you have to raise the performance of the group as a whole. Support the people you manage by first being civil and creating a personality or character that is trustworthy. Ask questions about procedures and equipment and look for suggestions that employees offer. Act upon those suggestions and improve their experience one bit at a time. Make the new culture where the standard is the higher performance of people. Make the new peer pressure be a higher standard of performance.

Situation #2: Poor Performance—Specifically, Task Completion Is Taking Too Long

On the surface, once again you might assume the poor performance is due to incompetence, but when you look a little deeper, you observe that it is actually due to employees being afraid to complete tasks because they think doing so will mean more work. How would you handle this situation?

Possible Response(s)

The experts on a job are the people that have been on the job for months, years, or even decades. You will never be an expert in all the positions you manage. You need to value that experience and support the people on those jobs. People over time have figured out the most efficient way of performing their job, and some people are afraid to show that their job has become streamlined, and fear that somebody will notice and use that opportunity to add work. When these people are asked questions on how to improve their job, they may be reluctant to offer information. Maybe their job cannot be improved much more. In this situation, ask questions from your observations, and learn how that person resolved their problems on their own. Let them know that they have achieved great success on their own and you would like to share that information with others to make their jobs better. Apply that process to other processes in your department and others will see that when you ask questions and make observations it is not always about how to possibly add work or make their job better, but that this process is making the work experience better for others as well.

Optional Assignment (Answers Will Vary; Discuss with Your Trainer and/or the Training Group)

Review the "Bear in the Woods" story and write a 1,000-word essay on what workplace culture conditions you think support or encourage this kind of mentality.

Bear in the Woods

This scenario is about survival of the fittest. The story is when two people are being chased by a bear in the woods, to survive you only have to be faster than the other person. This scenario can be applied to a group of employees in the same job description who are performing just enough to be ahead of the worst one or two employees. The thinking is that their job is safe as long as they perform just ahead of the worst one or two employees—"My job is safe as long as John and Carol are still here, they are struggling." When looking at poor performance, the questions you ask about improvements may not be offered or completely up-front. It is possible that valid answers to your questions are withheld until needed when they need to improve their performance. Also, answers to your questions may be withheld when the poor performers are asked because others do not want them to perform above their own level. The goal is to show that the communal discussions and suggestions should benefit the group. It is not a good work environment, or strategy, to achieve goals when not everybody is attaining them. The new environment should be that even though the relatively lower performers are at the bottom of the group, they are still hitting their goals and objectives set by the company. They would no longer be poor performers, but continuously improving performers, showing upward trends and benefitting the group as a whole.

Quiz Answers

1. "Transfer" of learning refers to:
   a. Sharing what you know with someone else
   b. **Using what you learn on the job**
   c. Mentoring
   d. Using skills from one job at the next job
2. If you are speaking to someone and his or her eyes start to wander, he or she looks away or lowers his or her head, this may be a sign that the person:
   a. is disappointed
   b. is disinterested
   c. **is distracted**
   d. does not like you
3. The main purpose of an assessment is to:
   a. **understand why things are how they are**
   b. identify how things should be
   c. figure out what needs to be changed
   d. sort employees based on competency
4. A good time to assess employee performance is:
   a. when employee is on a short, scheduled break
   b. before or after regular scheduled work hours
   c. **when employee is just finishing break**
   d. during employee's lunch period

Chapter 7—For Consideration

Question: Referencing the civility culture continuum chart below, at which stages/levels would you engage in feedback with employees?

Possible Response(s)

You would coach and/or give feedback at ALL levels. The timing and approach might vary but you provide feedback to all employees regardless of their level, i.e., both positive and negative scores.

Question: How much time should you spend with employees when giving feedback? Do you spend more time when addressing negative behavior?

Possible Response(s)

When you spend the exact amount of time on each person—regardless of where they are on the continuum—you are setting a consistent, standardized response. By not focusing on the nonperformers, you are not inadvertently engaging in a "reverse favoritism," i.e., giving attention and reward for bad behavior.

Question: An employee is sleeping on the job. You catch him. It's a 1-day suspension and he knows that he is caught. How do you manage this situation in a way that changes behavior but builds trust?

Possible Response(s)

Give the individual an opportunity to explain why the behavior happened. Do your job in terms of making sure the employee knows that the outcome could have been different, and that the behavior is not acceptable. Show that you are reasonable and that you are not interested in punishing just for the sake of punishing. Be sure to only use this approach when there is no harm done to the organization or another individual.

When it comes to safety issues, there is no tolerance or second chances.

A determined action is different than behavior. For example, smoking on the job is a behavior. Willfully putting on a wrong part or deliberately ignoring a workplace rule is determined action.

DON'T ASSUME that there is malice or some unfounded reason or rationale for the behavior, but wait to find out the reason. The individual might have a valid point or reason.

ASK WHY the person in engaging in the behavior. Try to start with a root cause approach and try to find out why the person is not performing appropriately.

Optional Assignment (Answers Will Vary; Discuss with Your Trainer and/or the Training Group)

Find three different examples of standard operating procedures (SOPs) from three different positions in manufacturing. Review the documents and make a list of all the components of information that you see are commonly recorded on an SOP.

Quiz Answers

1. What percentage of employees say the feedback they receive improves their work?
   a. 75 percent
   b. **26 percent**
   c. 14 percent
   d. 3 percent
2. Here are some examples of behaviors. Put a checkmark beside those which are determined actions and would require corrective action. **ALL SHOULD BE CHECK-MARKED.**
   - Putting the wrong taillight on
   - Arguing with a supervisor
   - Smoking in the plant
   - Being drunk or drinking on the job
   - Not wearing safety glasses when working with welding equipment
   - Being 4 minutes late for shift
   - Not doing what he or she was asked to do—this is the first time, e.g., move some steel coils from one part of the plant to another
   - Mistreating another employee, e.g., harassing a coworker
   - Using the incorrect tools
   - Taking a shortcut that will impact quality
   - Deliberately withholding information that will impact someone else negatively
   - Regularly engaging in shop talk or negativity
   - Stealing a piece of equipment or some supplies
   - Failing to interact effectively with coworkers
   - Not doing part of the job for the whole shift (missing parts or tools)
3. A communication tool that offers an opportunity for relationship building, tracking progress, and problem-solving is called:
   a. Variance
   b. Six Sigma
   c. Reliant measure
   d. **Feedback**

4. An SOP is:
   a. Standard Open Position
   b. Strategic Operating Plan
   c. Standing Only Procedure
   d. **Standard Operating Procedure**

Chapter 8—For Consideration

Key Questions to Ask to Initiate Interaction

A) Hello X, I just noticed (or Y mentioned), that you are not doing Z. Can you tell me why you are not doing Z?
B) Hi X, I wanted to check in and see how things are going. Let's take a few minutes and run through your job description.
C) X, we have changed/updated your job description so I want to ensure that you can do Z.

Some of the Responses You Might Get

1. **I don't have time to do Z.**

   Recommended response:

   > When is the last time you read your SOP?
   > Let's look at the SOP and see if you are following the steps.
   > As we read the SOP line by line, ask if you have any questions.

2. **I don't know how to do Z.**

   Recommended response:

   > Which part(s) of your job description do you not know how to do?
   > Do you need more training?
   > (The supervisor needs to confirm the responses, e.g., check if he/she was trained.)
   > If the person was trained, supervisor says, "What specific parts of the job do you need training in?"

3. **I wasn't trained to do Z.**

   Recommended response:

   > The supervisor says, "Okay, I will bring someone over to train you."

4. **Boss A told me to do Y instead of Z.**

   Recommended response:

   (Employees are told to follow their last instruction. So this is a legitimate response, and they should not be reprimanded or punished for doing so.)

5. **It's not my job to do Z.**

   Recommended response:

   Let's review the SOP or job description to verify that this is not part of your job. (For example, the stock someone needs is 30 feet away from the station, sequenced in five categories on a skid. It is another person's job to sequence the stock—he is out of parts a, b, c, and d. He has no item e, and it is someone else's job to sequence and sort the stock.)

   Supervisor should say, "You need to tell me when you can't do the job."

   Then make the box smaller by saying, "You need to tell me when you have just 15 pieces left."

6. **I can't do Z due to an injury.**

   Recommended response:

   What is your injury?
   How did the injury happen?
   When did the injury happen?

7. **I don't have permission to do Z.**

   Recommended response:

   The task is within your job description so I am giving you permission.

8. **I don't have the right tools to do Z.**

   Recommended response:

   What tools exactly do you need? (Sometimes they have the tools, but they are not working at 100 percent.)

9. **If I do Z, then X will happen.**

   Recommended response:

   And what is the consequence of that?
   What would you do instead?

10. **I would do Z except I don't want to help Y.**

    Recommended response:

    Why don't you want to help Y?
    (Often the reason is, "It's not fair that I do my job 100 percent and then I have to help someone else do his or her job.") Supervisors who are paying attention will pick up on this and say, "Go do your job and address him versus me."

11. **If I help Y, I can't get my own work done.**

    Recommended response:

    So what work should you be doing and what is pulling you away from those tasks? Possible answer might be, "I can't even do what I'm supposed to do, how am I going to help him or her?" or "Well, I have to walk 100 feet to find a printer that works." (Recommendation here is to fix the printer.)

12. **This is a new upgrade.**

    Recommended response:

    Were you not informed of the new process?
    Did you not receive training?

13. **I know what to do but I'm not doing it.**

    Recommended response:

    Why won't you do it?

14. **It's not safe to do what you are asking.**

    Recommended response:

    Specifically, what is unsafe?

Optional Assignment (Answers Will Vary; Discuss with Your Trainer and/or the Training Group)

Review the thinking skills assessments and rate yourself. Then write a personal learning plan outlining any thinking skills you need to develop. Include how you will acquire the skills, e.g., courses, resources etc.

Section 1: Self-Assessment

PROBLEM-SOLVING			
I can...	Yes	Somewhat	No
Identify the cause of a problem when I have all the necessary information given to me.			
Follow existing procedures or instructions to identify solutions to a problem (e.g., the steps for fixing a broken machine).			
Find information from a variety of sources (such as equipment manuals, policies, and procedures) that will help me understand the problem and identify solutions.			
Use problem-solving experiences I had in the past to help me identify solutions to current problems.			
Recognize key facts and issues related to a problem (e.g., identify answers to who, what, when, where, why, and how).			
Identify and evaluate the pros and cons of each potential solution.			
Make adjustments to existing workplace procedures to help solve a problem (set procedures may not address every type of problem).			
Evaluate how well a solution worked.			

Figure 20 Problem Solving Self-Assessment, Masotti 2019

Section 2: Personal Development

Completing this section will help you identify your strengths and areas that you may want to improve with regard to your thinking skills. You can use this information to help develop your training plans.

Thinking Strengths

Look at the "Yes" column in **Section 1** for each thinking skill to identify your strengths and record them below.

I am confident that I can...
e.g. apply past experiences to new problems or decisions.

1. _____

2. _____

3. _____

Tip: Consider using your strengths to help a coworker, friend, or family member improve their **thinking** skills.

Areas for Improvement

Look at the "Somewhat" and/or "No" columns in **Section 1** for each thinking skill to identify the areas that you need to develop or strengthen and record them below.

I would like to improve my ability to...

e.g. make sure that minor interruptions do not interfere with my work plans.

1. _____

2. _____

3. _____

Tip: When developing your training plan, focus on improving one or two thinking skills tasks at a time.

Quiz Answers

1. "Variability" is...
   a. **inconsistencies, changes, or options in a typical situation or context**
   b. the way things change in a geographical area
   c. how people adapt to change
   d. the degree to which change can be managed

2. Step 2 in the "make the box smaller" method is…
   a. embed civility
   b. observe
   c. **set expectations**
   d. monitor and measure
   e. provide feedback

3. To change workplace culture, it is a good idea to give feedback how often?
   a. Once a week
   b. Once a year
   c. **Once a day**
   d. Once a month

4. Civility Experts Inc. field research shows that what percentage of variability related to solving people problems falls in the outside/largest "box" and is related to trust?
   a. 15 percent
   b. 8 percent
   c. 75 percent
   d. **50 percent**

CHAPTER 10

Tools You Can Use

Waste is worse than loss. The time is coming when every person who lays claim to ability will keep the question of waste before him constantly. The scope of thrift is limitless.

—Thomas Edison

General Information and Related to Introduction

Glossary of Common Generic Manufacturing Terms[1]

(Unless indicated otherwise, all definitions are from Simplicable.com)

Assembly line is a type of production line that produces an assembly of parts and components. At each step, parts or components are added bringing the product closer to being fully assembled.

Authentic honesty: When a person tells the truth because being honest is one of his or her core values and doing so is the right and good thing to do, this is **authentic honesty**. In this case, though, partly because the truth-telling is values-based, the truth teller considers the *way* the truth comes out, e.g., considering what is appropriate timing, giving the listener some warning etc.—LB.

Automation is the use of largely automatic equipment in a system of manufacturing or other production processes (Google Dictionary).

Behavior is what people do or say—it is typically observable, measurable, and reliable. Behavior is NOT feelings, motives, or traits.—LB

Benchmarking is the process of comparing your results to those of peers in your industry. It is an essential business activity that is key to

---

[1]Simplicable. April 16, 2016. "30 Manufacturing Terms." https://simplicable.com/new/manufacturing.04/05/2019

understanding competitive advantages and disadvantages. In some cases, benchmarking results are also used in promotion and sales materials. The following are illustrative examples of benchmarking.

Blind obedience refers to when an employee expresses an objection to a directive when told to do something by a supervisor, but follows orders. Objection could be verbal or nonverbal, and often comes across as stubborn or insubordinate because the employee doesn't always give a reason for not wanting to follow the direction. Blind obedience might be observed as vocalizing, "okay boss" or, "whatever you say" or "you sure" with a doubtful or questioning tone, eyeball rolling, raised eyebrows etc.—CM

Bottleneck is a hindrance to productivity, efficiency, or speed. The term is an analogy to the shape of a bottle that narrows at the neck. A bottleneck is typically a component of a process that is slower than everything that depends on it.

Brain-restraint is psychological pause. This means suspending judgment and avoiding jumping to conclusions. Of course, your general brain activity doesn't stop; the idea is that you deliberately stall aspects of your thinking patterns or habits. For just a few minutes, don't think. Experience and observe calmly and keep a neutral mindset.—CM

Civility is a conscious awareness of the impact of one's thoughts, actions, words, and intentions on others, combined with a continuous acknowledgement of one's responsibility to ease the experience of others (e.g., through restraint, kindness, non-judgment, respect, and courtesy), and a consistent effort to adopt and exhibit civil behavior as a non-negotiable point of one's character.—LB

Command and control: This power-focused management style when applied to manufacturing is called "command and control." In a command and control[2] style, a properly designated leader or commander exercises authority and directs subordinates.

Continual improvement is a broader term preferred by W. Edwards Deming to refer to general processes of improvement and encompassing "discontinuous" improvements—that is, many different approaches, covering different areas.

---

[2]The Free Dictionary (Farlex). February, 2012. "Command and Control." www.thefreedictionary.com/command and control. 05/05/2019

Continuous improvement is a subset of continual improvement, with a more specific focus on linear, incremental improvement within an existing process. Some practitioners also associate *continuous improvement* more closely with techniques of statistical process control.

Continuous improvement is understood to be a deliberate, planned (and sometimes strategic), ongoing effort to improve products, services, or processes.

Continuous learning refers to the ability to continually develop and improve one's skills and knowledge in order to perform effectively and adapt to changes in the workplace.[3]

Cultural competence is the ability to understand, communicate with, and effectively interact with people across cultures. Cultural competence encompasses being aware of one's own world view, developing positive attitudes towards cultural differences, and gaining knowledge of different cultural practices and world views.[4]

Culture is defined as how we REALLY do things in an organization, i.e., irrespective of policy, behaviors and approaches become the accepted experience.—CM

Culture indicator continuum is an assessment tool devised by Masotti & Bayer in 2019. The tool enables organizations to understand how common behaviors observed on the manufacturing floor (and/or in other workplaces) correlate with overall measures of civility.

Cycle time is the duration of a business process from start to end. This can be used as a metric to manage processes. Alternatively, it can be used to plan and improve operations such as a production line. Cycle time is defined in the context of a business or industry.

DMAIC refers to a data-driven improvement cycle used for improving, optimizing, and stabilizing business processes and designs. The DMAIC improvement cycle is the core tool used to drive Six Sigma

---

[3]Essential Skills Expert Review Panel. February 14, 2012. "What Do You Think of This Idea?: Review of Definition for Continuous Learning." https://essentialskills .ideascale.com/a/dtd/Review-of-definition-for-Continuous-Learning/94638-17651 .04/05/2019

[4]http://makeitourbusiness.ca/blog/what-does-it-mean-be-culturally-competent .05/05/2019

projects. However, DMAIC is not exclusive to Six Sigma and can be used as the framework for other improvement applications.[5]

Emotional intelligence has been defined, by Peter Salovey and John Mayer, as "the ability to monitor one's own and other people's emotions, to discriminate between different emotions and label them appropriately, and to use emotional information to guide thinking and behavior."

End-in-mind listening: This is a civility term referring to going into communications knowing in advance of the conversation what you need to happen *after* the communication. Because you know what your end goal is, you may relinquish control of how you get to the desired end point; for example, you don't assume you know how people will respond, but because the interaction is goal-directed communication, you can ask strategic questions. By using an end-in-mind listening approach, you will usually get the answers you need quickly and precisely. At the same time, you build trust because your motives are transparent and you are direct and fact-based.—LB

Engagement refers to intentional, conscious "buying-in" on the part of employees such that because they trust the organization, they choose to come to work, contribute in a meaningful way, do more than they are required to, support their coworkers, and believe in what the organization stands for and is trying to achieve, even when things are difficult.—LB

Enterprise resource planning is defined as the ability to deliver an integrated suite of business applications. ERP tools share a common process and data model, covering broad and deep operational end-to-end processes, such as those found in finance, HR, distribution, manufacturing, service, and the supply chain.[6]

Feedback is a communication tool that offers an opportunity for relationship building, tracking progress, and problem-solving.

Hardiness refers to your physical stamina, your ability to endure harsh conditions and maintain a standard of performance.—CM

Idiosyncratic rater effect: That our evaluations are deeply colored by our own understanding of what we're rating others on, our own sense

---

[5] Wikimedia Foundation. May 6, 2020. "DMAIC," *Wikipedia*. https://en.wikipedia.org/wiki/DMAIC. 05/05/2019

[6] Gartner_Inc. n.d. "Enterprise Resource Planning (ERP)," *Gartner*. www.gartner.com/en/information-technology/glossary/enterprise-resource-planning-erp. 04/06/2019

of what good looks like for a particular competency, our harshness or leniency as raters, and our own inherent and unconscious biases is called "idiosyncratic rater effect."

Industrial revolution refers to the changes in manufacturing and transportation that began with fewer things being made by hand but instead made using machines in larger-scale factories.[7]

Internet of things entails the interconnection of unique devices within an existing Internet infrastructure, to achieve a variety of goals including cost reduction, increased efficiency, improved safety, meeting compliance requirements, and product innovation. IoT's existence is primarily due to three factors: widely available Internet access, smaller sensors, and cloud computing.

Karoshi which can be translated literally as "overwork death" in Japanese, is occupational sudden mortality.

Key performance indicators: A performance indicator or key performance indicator is a type of performance measurement. KPIs evaluate the success of an organization or of a particular activity in which it engages.

Knowledge worker is defined as an employee who may know how to do aspects of many jobs, who is a continuous learner, and who takes responsibility for his or her own learning.

Light industry is any manufacturing or construction industry that doesn't involve heavy and capital intensive products or production equipment. The term heavy industry is reserved for the most capital intensive of all industries. Most manufacturers are considered light industry.

Mass production is the production of goods at scale typically using a production line. It differs from other forms of production in that all steps in the production process are run concurrently and continuously.

Needs assessment is a systematic exploration of the way things are and the way they should be. These "things" are usually associated with organizational and/or individual performance.

---

[7]Yourdictionary. n.d. "Industrial Revolution,"www.yourdictionary.com/industrial-revolution.05/06/2019

The purpose of conducting a needs assessment is to better understand the reason why things are the way they are, rather than the way they should be and/or how we want them to be.

Off-standard behavior references a situation, behavior, gesture, approach, etc. that is not typical, that is, different from what you have come to understand as normal or standard.—CM

People treatment is a civility term that refers to an overall attitude about what constitutes a fair and good way of interacting with people. It includes how you speak, nonverbal gestures, the extent to which you are empathetic, and how you define honesty and integrity. An individual's idea of people treatment can vary from one context to another.—LB

Persona: The qualities and characteristics that you create or build in an effort to fit into a particular situation or role are your **persona**. For example, if you are not a "rough" person by nature, you might adopt language, gestures, or specific postures as a way of projecting sameness with the people around you.—CM

Positive workplace culture happens when what really happens is in fact the expected experience.—CM

Principled disobedience refers to when an employee expresses an objection to a directive and explains that he or she does not want to do what he or she is told based on his or her view that the action does not align with the organization's policy related to quality or standard. Principled disobedience might be observed as an employee vocalizing, "I don't want to do/won't do what you ask because doing so will result in a product that is of inferior quality and not what organization X does/endorses," or "I can't do what you ask because it is not up to company X standard, or will take more time than allowable or will cost too much."—CM

Protective disobedience is when an employee expresses an objection to a directive and explains that he or she does not want to do/will not do what he or she is told based on his or her view that the action creates an unsafe condition for him or her or for his or her coworkers. Protective disobedience might be observed as an employee vocalizing, "I cannot/will not do as you ask because it is unsafe."—CM

Quality control is the process of detecting mistakes in the production of products and delivery of services. It is a process of ensuring that things meet their functional requirements, non-functional requirements, and detailed specifications. Quality control may test every product produced and every service interaction. Alternatively, quality control may test representative samples.

Relational wealth is a civility term used by Civility Experts Inc. that refers to the invaluable benefits of strong connections via interpersonal relationships. Relational wealth relates to Civility Experts Inc. CEO, Lew Bayer's suggestion that "collaboration is currency in the new world of work."—LB

Resilience refers to mental stamina and the ability to bounce back, to regain composure and control, and to move forward in a solutions-focused way. It requires personal strength, grit, fidelity of character, and a positive outlook.—CM

Respectful workplace policy are policies intended to direct processes and protocol related to perceived inappropriate treatment including bullying or harassment.

Restraint is a physical halt or pause used in the Masotti Common-sense Social Competence Strategy "wait for it." The halt may include a verbal pause, being quiet, holding still, and/or showing restraint by taking no action for a measured amount of time.—CM

Retention refers to how many employees/hires are "kept" or maintained at the organization—do not quit, or be fired or laid off.

Reverse social engineering is a social radar strategy where you observe behavior and make mental or other notes about what you see. Then, when situations or communications don't go as planned, you work backwards. Start with the outcome and recall the gestures, words, tone, and cues that should have hinted or warned you that the exchange was off track. This enables you to recognize those cues in future so that you can adjust your approach as necessary and avoid the undesired outcome.—CM

Righteous honesty: When someone is taking an indignant or defensive stance and so blurts out hurtful honesty, i.e. tells the truth about someone else's actions as a means of deflecting attention from his or her own dishonesty, that person is engaging in righteous honesty.—LB

Sales and operations planning (S&OP) is the process of coordinating marketing and operations. It is designed to align demand processes such as sales, promotion, and distribution with supply process such as service delivery, supply chain, and manufacturing. S&OP is an iterative process that often revolves around monthly or weekly sales volume forecasts.

Shared information bias refers to how individuals in a nice workplace learn that one of the best ways of making a group feel good and making their teammates see them as competent is to repeat and repackage information that everyone already knows. Shared information bias makes the person sharing look smart and in-step with his or her colleagues, even if he or she is just rehashing the same thing that was said last week or by a person who spoke a moment prior.—Quartz

Situational blindness is the inability to see what is right in front of you in a workplace setting. Situational blindness typically results from low social radar skills and can result in spending unnecessary time doing, or thinking about, things that need not be done at all. In manufacturing, an example is when a supervisor fails to consider that the members of his team likely have the answers to a problem he is trying to solve and so rather than ask his team, he spends a lot of time looking for answers that are right in front of him.—CM

Six Sigma is a set of techniques and tools for process improvement. It was introduced by American engineer Bill Smith while working at Motorola in 1986.

Social acuity is a term used by Civility Experts Inc. that describes the level of accuracy and consistency with which a person can apply his or her social intelligence, i.e. the sharpness of a person's perception of the overall tone of a room or the unspoken messages, or the "feel" of a scenario is an indication of his or her social acuity.—LB

Social competence is related to civility at work; specifically, social competence is a cluster of skills including those below. To be competent socially, an individual is able to apply all of the skills below concurrently and consistently which results in the ability to communicate and interact in a way that builds positive, trusting relationships.—LB

- Social intelligence
- Personal management basics

- Resilience
- Hardiness
- Cultural competence

Social honesty: When a person says what is perceived to be the right thing in a certain context, even when it isn't polite to tell the truth, or when telling the truth is not politically correct or could harm social impression or status, he or she is engaging in social honesty.—LB

Social intelligence refers to one of four skills that underpin the ability to be civil, according to Civility Experts Inc. Social intelligence is a cluster of three subskills (social style, social radar, and social knowledge) and one of several intelligences, e.g., kinesthetic, emotional, mathematical, etc. Social intelligence is your ability to effectively read and interpret nonverbal, verbal, tonal, and contextual cues in a range of social settings. Social intelligence is critical to building trust and to forming long-lasting relationships.—LB

SOP refers to a Standard Operating Procedure.

Team knowledge is information about a workplace, e.g., processes, short cuts, personnel, unwritten rules, etc., that are only learned when on the job.

Team skills are skills that are learned while "living in a workplace culture," e.g., information, skills, habits, techniques, etc. that are learned (and usually contained) on the job.—CM

Toxic culture refers to the presence of various symptoms of incivility. The extent to which a workplace is uncivil would present that culture as toxic or harmful to the employees.

Transfer of learning is the extent to which an employee or learner is able to use what he or she learned in training when he or she goes back to work, i.e. proof of learning shown by practicing the new skill on the job.—LB

Transistor is a semiconductor device used to amplify or switch electronic signals and electrical power. It is composed of semiconductor material usually with at least three terminals for connection to an external circuit.

Trident Approach is a three-pronged approach to embedding civility into organizations as a continuous improvement strategy.—CM

Trust can be defined as a personal comfort or psychological safety about a person or event, concept, piece of information, process etc.—LB

Variability is the extent of change or difference from a designated start of an event or process to a designated point in the process. It might refer to any "off-standard" condition.—CM

Workplace culture: The habits, traditions, attitudes, tone of interactions, and general behaviors that make up employees' day-to-day experience on the job make up what can be described as workplace culture. An individual experiences workplace culture by living in the workplace. And because we typically interact with, and impact, those we work with, the people living in the organization co-create the workplace culture.—CM/LB

In Case You Didn't Know—Some Stats and Facts about the Manufacturing Industry, USA and Global. www.nam.org/ Newsroom/Top-20-Facts-About-Manufacturing/

Canada:

- Auto manufacturing regularly contributes over $20 billion to Canada's GDP.
- Nationally, auto and parts production accounts for about 16.8 percent of manufacturing sales.
- In Ontario, transportation equipment manufacturing is 20.2 percent of GDP.
- Direct industry employment in Canada accounts for 130,000. jobs.
- Manufacturing is a cornerstone of our modern economy. Accounting for approximately $174 billion of our GDP, manufacturing represents more than 10 percent of Canada's total GDP. What is more, manufacturers export more than $354 billion each year, representing 68 percent of all of Canada's merchandise exports.
  - All of this adds up to 1.7 million quality full-time, well-paying jobs—all across the country. And as the sector has modernized, manufacturers have become innovative and high-tech, relying on a highly skilled and knowledgeable workforce that includes designers, researchers, programmers, engineers, technicians, and tradespeople.

○ Canada's manufacturing industry has huge potential for its economic future. The world is changing, and new technologies are not just opening new markets for Canadian goods, they are changing the ways these goods are produced. For manufacturing in Canada to remain a vibrant, innovative, and competitive contributor to our economy, business and government will need to work together. A vibrant manufacturing community encourages industrial clusters that develop skills, knowledge, and technology. Success breeds success: when Canada's manufacturers grow and compete, they act as magnets for new investment and for new young people wanting to be part of this great industry, making the products of tomorrow.

• Canada is one of the few developed nations that is a net exporter of energy—in 2009, net exports of energy products amounted to 2.9 percent of the GDP. Most important are the large oil and gas resources centered in Alberta and the Northern Territories, but also present in neighboring British Columbia and Saskatchewan. The vast Athabasca oil sands give Canada the world's third largest reserves of oil after Saudi Arabia and Venezuela according to USGS. In British Columbia and Quebec, as well as Ontario, Saskatchewan, Manitoba, and the Labrador region, hydroelectric power is an inexpensive and relatively environmental—friendly source of abundant energy. In part because of this, Canada is also one of the world's highest per capita consumers of energy. Cheap energy has enabled the creation of several important industries, such as the large aluminum industries in British Columbia and Quebec.[8]

Some Excellent Reading If You Want to Learn More about Manufacturing

• *The Design of Everyday Things*: Revised and Expanded Edition Paperback—November 5, 2013 by Don Norman (Author)

---

[8]Canada's Manufacturing Sector. 2020. "Canadian Manufacturing Sector Gateway," *Innovation, Science and Economic Development Canada*. https://ic.gc.ca/eic/site/mfg-fab.nsf/eng/home (Modified March 12, 2020).

- *The Lean Six Sigma Pocket Toolbook: A Quick Reference Guide to 100 Tools for Improving Quality and Speed* by George, Rowlands, Price and Maxey (Authors)
- *The Toyota Way: 14 Management Principles from the World's Greatest Manufacturer* Hardcover—January 7, 2004 by Jeffrey K. Liker (Author)
- *Lean—Lean Startup, Lean Analytics, Lean Enterprise, Kaizen, Six Sigma, Agile Project Management*, Kanban, Scrum, Kaizen by Jason Bennett (Author), Jennifer Bowen (Author), Eric LaCord (Narrator), Jennifer Bowen Jason Bennett (Publisher)

Sample Job Description

Production supervisor job responsibilities:

Supervises products by manufacturing staff, organizing and monitoring workflow.

Production supervisor job duties:

- Accomplishes manufacturing staff results by communicating job expectations; planning, monitoring, and appraising job results; coaching, counseling, and disciplining employees; initiating, coordinating, and enforcing systems, policies, and procedures.
- Maintains staff by recruiting, selecting, orienting, and training employees; developing personal growth opportunities.
- Maintains workflow by monitoring steps of the process; setting processing variables; observing control points and equipment; monitoring personnel and resources; studying methods; implementing cost reductions; developing reporting procedures and systems; facilitating corrections to malfunctions within process control points; initiating and fostering a spirit of cooperation within and between departments.
- Completes production plan by scheduling and assigning personnel; accomplishing work results; establishing priorities; monitoring progress; revising schedules; resolving problems; reporting results of the processing flow on shift production summaries.

- Maintains quality service by establishing and enforcing organization standards.
- Ensures operation of equipment by calling for repairs; evaluating new equipment and techniques.
- Provides manufacturing information by compiling, initiating, sorting, and analyzing production performance records and data; answering questions and responding to requests.
- Creates and revises systems and procedures by analyzing operating practices, record-keeping systems, forms of control, and budgetary and personnel requirements; implementing change.
- Maintains safe and clean work environment by educating and directing personnel on the use of all control points, equipment, and resources; maintaining compliance with established policies and procedures.
- Maintains working relationship with the union by following the terms of the collective bargaining agreement.
- Resolves personnel problems by analyzing data; investigating issues; identifying solutions; recommending action.
- Maintains professional and technical knowledge by attending educational workshops; reviewing professional publications; establishing personal networks; benchmarking state-of-the-art practices; participating in professional societies.
- Contributes to team effort by accomplishing related results as needed.

Production supervisor skills and qualifications:

Supervision, coaching, managing processes, process improvement, tracking budget expenses, production planning, controls and instrumentation, strategic planning, dealing with complexity, financial planning and strategy, automotive manufacturing

Essential Skills Pre-Training Evaluation

Adapted from Workplace Education Manitoba and Gov.gc.ca (assesses working with others, thinking skills, and oral communication).

Oral Communication Self-Assessment—Check the Box That Applies to You.

I can...	Yes	Somewhat	No
Ask routine questions to obtain information			
Understand short messages and communicate the information to others			
Give simple instructions or facts to others on a familiar topic			
Listen to others without interrupting			
Use appropriate body language (e.g., smiling, nodding, making eye contact) while having a conversation			
Ask complex questions to get the appropriate information			
Communicate with others to resolve minor conflicts, such as customer complaints			
Communicate with others to coordinate work or resolve problems			
Express my opinions and ideas clearly and concisely			
Restate information that is presented orally			
Train or give clear instructions to a coworker			
Give a brief presentation to a small group			
Lead routine meetings (e.g., weekly team meetings)			
Follow complex oral instructions to complete a task			
Explain difficult subject matter using detailed examples			
Give yourself 3 points for every Yes, 2 points for every Somewhat and 1 point for every No.			
Total			

Figure 21 Oral Communication Self-Assessment©, Workplace Education Manitoba 2014

Total possible score is 45. If your score is lower than 37, it is recommended that you upgrade your essential skills.

Working with Others Self-Assessment—Check the Box That Applies to You.

I can....	Yes	Somewhat	No
Organize my work tasks within a set of priorities			
Take initiative by doing what needs to be done before being asked			
Work cooperatively with a partner or team to complete tasks			
Coordinate my work with the work of my colleagues to complete group projects			
Complete my assigned work on time so that team deadlines are met			
Complete my fair share of tasks when working with a partner or team			
Follow directions from my partner or team members as required			
Give directions to my partner or team members as required			
Participate in making group decisions by contributing my ideas and suggestions			
Contribute to making decisions cooperatively and settling differences respectfully			
Improve my work based on suggestions and advice I receive from my partner or other team members			
Help build an open and trustworthy work environment by encouraging others to participate in activities			
Lead by setting a good example for the people around me			
Make decisions that I feel others can respect			
Provide constructive feedback to help others improve their work			
Take the lead in coordinating my colleagues' tasks in a group project			
Encourage group interactions and maintain a positive atmosphere within my team			
Give yourself 3 points for every Yes, 2 points for every Somewhat and 1 point for every No.			
Total			

Figure 22 Working with Others Self-Assessment©, Workplace Education Manitoba 2014

Total possible score is 51. If your score is lower than 43, it is recommended that you upgrade your essential skills.

Thinking Skills Self-Assessment—Check the Box That Applies to You.

I can....	Yes	Somewhat	No
Identify the cause of a problem when I have all the necessary information given to me			
Follow existing procedures or instructions to identify solutions to a problem (e.g., the steps for fixing a broken machine)			
Find information from a variety of sources (such as equipment manuals, policies, and procedures) that will help me understand the problem and identify solutions			
Use problem-solving experiences I had in the past to help me identify solutions to current problems			
Recognize key facts and issues related to a problem (e.g., identify answers to who, what, when, where, why, and how)			
Identify and evaluate the pros and cons of each potential solution			
Make adjustments to existing workplace procedures to help solve a problem (set procedures may not address every type of problem)			
Evaluate how well a solution worked			
Make decisions when following existing procedures or policies			
Use my knowledge and past experiences to help me make decisions			
Consider all the relevant information available before making a decision			
Decide which of several options is most appropriate			
Explain why I chose a particular decision			
Complete tasks by their level of importance that have been organized for me			
Complete tasks by their level of importance that I have organized on my own			
Use tools such as calendars, agendas, and to-do lists to help me organize my tasks			
Coordinate my work with the work of my coworkers (e.g., make a schedule for using a shared piece of equipment)			
Deal with interruptions so that they do not interfere with my work schedule			
Give yourself 3 points for every Yes, 2 points for every Somewhat and 1 point for every No.			
Total			

Figure 23 Thinking Skills Self-Assessment©, Workplace Education Manitoba 2014

Total possible score is 54: If your score is lower than 46, it is recommended that you update your essential skills.

Chapter 1

Research Reveals the 4 Top Trends in Manufacturing at the macro level (across different kinds of manufacturing):

- Robotics/Artificial intelligence
- Lean processes/Supply chain optimization
- Digitization, 3-D printing, and demand for tech-savvy employees
- Spending on security

Specific aspects and details about how various types of manufacturing will be impacted by the above are indicated below—please see links in footnote for more information.

- Clothing and textiles. Companies that process raw wool, cotton, and flax to make cloth are categorized under the clothing and textiles sector.[9]
- Petroleum, chemicals, and plastics[10]
- Electronics, computers, and transportation[11]
- Food production[12]
- Metal manufacturing[13]
- Wood, leather, and paper[14]

---

[9] S. Kochar. March 18, 2020. "5 Top Trends in Fashion Manufacturing Technology," *Techpacker Blog*. www.techpacker.com/blog/5-top-trends-in-fashion-manufacturing-technology/.

[10] S. Wadyalkar. July 23, 2018. "3 Megatrends in the Chemical Industry," *Market Research Blog*. https://blog.marketresearch.com/3-megatrends-in-the-chemical-industry.

[11] Hitachi Solutions. February 7, 2019. "10 Trends That Will Dominate Manufacturing Trends in 2019." https://us.hitachi-solutions.com/blog/top-manufacturing-trends/.

[12] Foodprocessing.com. n.d. "Manufacturing Trends." www.foodprocessing.com/category/manufacturing_trends/.

[13] Mainstay Manufacturing. October 4, 2018. "Metal Fabrication Trends in 2018." https://mainstaymfg.com/metal-fabrication-trends-in-2018/.

[14] The Business Research Company. n.d. "Paper, Plastics, Rubber, Wood and Textile Manufacturing Industry Overview." www.thebusinessresearchcompany.com/industry/paper,-plastics,-rubber,-wood-and-textile-manufacturing-research.

Definition of Civility

CIVILITY is:

- a conscious awareness of the impact of one's thoughts, actions, words, and intentions on others; combined with,
- a continuous acknowledgement of one's responsibility to ease the experience of others (e.g., through restraint, kindness, non-judgment, respect, and courtesy); and,
- a consistent effort to adopt and exhibit civil behavior as a non-negotiable point of one's character.[15]
  —Lewena Bayer, CEO, Civility Experts Inc.

The Workplace Civility Metrics Survey® by Masotti and Bayer, 2019

Element	Average score 0 (–) and 10 (+)
Retention—general/overall	
Organizational capacity, e.g., maximizing resources	
Employee autonomy, e.g., at production level	
Individual skills mastery and confidence	
Effective goal setting, e.g., at production level	
Alignment of daily activity with organizational goals	
Accountability—generally	
Consistency in service delivery	
Respect in the workplace, e.g., if respect = value, to what extent was each individual valued equally?	
Exhibition of common courtesies	
Generalized reciprocity, i.e., doing for others with no expectation of return, and doing things that are not required by the job description	

Figure 24 Workplace Civility Metrics Survey® by Masotti and Bayer, 2019

---

[15]Civility Experts Inc. August 22, 2019. "Civility Experts Worldwide—Winnipeg Manitoba Canada." www.civilityexperts.com/.

Element	Average score 0 (−) and 10 (+)
Civil discourse, e.g., monitored tone, appropriate turn-taking, moderate volume, avoidance of harsh words or profanity	
Acceptance of diversity	
Team-orientation without being constantly directed to be a team	
Volunteer collaboration	
Innovation	
Thinking skills, e.g., effective decision-making, measured risk-taking	
Self-respect, e.g., standing up for what one believes is right (courage on the job)	
Self-directed learning, e.g., making independent choices to seek learning	
Culture of learning—encouraged by leaders and peers to pursue learning	
Change readiness—open to change and able to adapt in timely and effective way	
Engagement—defined as personal "buy-in" and trust of organization	
Understanding of shared purpose	
Overall trust	
Responsibility-taking without having to be directed, e.g., claiming errors or apologizing	
Self-rated happy-at-work scores	
Hardiness, e.g., physical bounce-back ability to withstand high physical stress	
Psychological safety, e.g., extent to which employee would feel okay stating personal issue related to health or otherwise	
Stress management, e.g., did company offer supports?	
Restraint, e.g., did people stop and think before taking action?	
Overall morale	
Efficient (timely and concise) communication	

Figure 24 Continued

Covey—Speed of Trust Survey Tools.

www.speedoftrust.com/speed-of-trust-measurement-tools

The Civility Culture Compass

www.civilityexperts.com/training-solutions/civility-workplace-assessments/

The Civility Culture Compass© devised by the team at Civility Experts Worldwide Inc. measures an organization relative to four conditions that need to be present and stable to ensure success of a civility initiative. These are:

- Change
- Engagement
- Readiness: logistical and skills-wise
- Alignment

Change: What is going on—past, present, and anticipated?

Engagement: How much do people choose to buy in? (Closely related to trust)

Alignment: To what extent do the day-to-day activities align with the strategic goals?

Readiness: How prepared, resources and skills-wise, is the organization to implement change?

The outcomes also hint at which, if any, of the core competencies underpin an ability to be civil. These are:

- Cultural competence
- Systems thinking
- Continuous learning
- Social intelligence

For more information and to use the free Civility Culture Compass Tool visit www.civilityexperts.com

Chapter 2

About the Trident

The Trident Approach to foster civility in day-to-day supervisor communications was devised by Christian Masotti and is based on the experience of 20+ years in manufacturing.

The trident is a three-pronged approach to managing SOPs, job descriptions, and daily performance that impacts culture, engagement, and bottom line metrics.

The key benefits to using the Trident Approach are:

- Supervisors all approach tasks such as managing standard operating procedures, reviewing job tasks, daily performance check-ins, Kaizen meetings, giving feedback and doing corrective action in the same general way, i.e. there is a recognized process to follow.
- Employees come to understand that the supervisors' roles and the activities, questions, behaviors, etc. that supervisors engage in are just processes that support the production system. As the behaviors become consistent, employees see supervisors as less threatening and come to understand that the supervisor's role is really to support the employee and make his or her ability to meet production KPIs easier.
- General exchanges between supervisors, employees, and others are less harsh. There is less fear of engaging with each other, more preparedness, less wasted time, less stress overall, and when things work well, there is increased trust, collaboration, and engagement.

Prong 1 of the Trident is Civil Communication Training. Leaders at all levels are trained first. This training focuses on teaching managers and supervisors "how" to engage, i.e. incorporating civility into tone, word choice, and demeanor. The strategy incorporates social intelligence aspects including social radar, social style, and social knowledge.

Civil communication training might include:

- What tone of voice is, what creates tone, what various tones mean, and how to monitor tone
- Words that undermine credibility
- Words and phrases that build trust and convey transparency
- Action-oriented words that encourage action
- End-in-mind communication
- How to match nonverbal communication to verbal, e.g., to reinforce a mood/tone
- How to read nonverbal cues, e.g., what do certain gestures mean
- Aspects of communication that are common depending on gender, generation, and cultural background

- What language is considered profanity
- How to avoid and/or respond to shop talk
- How to ask questions in a way that does not come across as accusatory
- How to show interest in others
- How to ask up to seven types of questions and when to ask them
- Language and approach for persuasion
- How to be tactful when giving bad news
- How to give directions with clarity
- How to avoid being parental
- How to convey specific directions, e.g., when behavior is required
- How to address inappropriate behavior
- How to restrain oneself, e.g., avoid being reactive
- How to monitor pace, pitch, and rhythm of voice to hold someone's attention
- How to communicate when there is impairment, e.g., visual or auditory issues
- How to communicate sensitive issues
- The difference between discussion, debate, and decision
- And so on....

Assessments can be completed such that not every individual has to go through all the training. \It is cost- and time-effective to do proper assessments and then train only to the gaps. The exception would be an orientation to a "culture of civility" training session where the mission, values, definitions, expectations, and related details about the civility initiative are conveyed to the entire work team—companywide would be ideal, but this is not always possible.

Prong 2 of the Trident is about Observation and Assessment. Specifically, leaders must be taught how to properly assess current condition, culture, and practices including where, when, why, and how incivility is present, and then they need to apply their civil communication knowledge and monitor the impact when they communicate and act with civility—this improvement should be tracked and reviewed. Once it is evident where incivility needs to be addressed, find out where the points of lowest trust are with the work team, start there. This step can incorporate a typical Plan-Do-Correct-Act approach.

Prong 3 is Applying the Masotti Feedback Method. A supervisor's ability to give feedback is critical and when applied consistently and effectively can have a lasting positive impact on an organization. It is a four-step process:

1. Lead with presence, civility, and social intelligence. E.g., the leader MUST exhibit the behavior he or she expects of his or her team. This means going into feedback settings with a civil mindset:
   - Share perspective with the employee; be empathetic when required, be kind when you can, and be direct and honest always.
   - See feedback as a coaching opportunity where you are engaging the employee, and encouraging learning versus taking a corrective or disciplining tone.
   - Be fair. Follow the same process regardless of who you are interacting with. Consistency is key to credibility with a feedback process.
2. Observe current communication and feedback practices; e.g., to assess needs, apply "Masotti Make the Box Smaller Process."
3. Interrupt current practice and use AEIOU method.
   The AEIOU method is a process for reviewing SOPs and job descriptions devised by Christian Masotti. The method incorporates social intelligence, organizational cultural competence, and continuous improvement considerations. The duration and frequency of the feedback is a critical component of the Masotti Method.
4. Coach the next level to use the Trident.

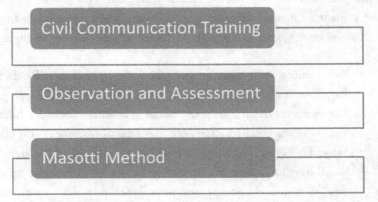

Figure 25 The Trident©, Masotti, 2019

Perspectives on Change—Quick self-Assessment

I believe that...	Yes	Somewhat	No
1. Change is inevitable.			
2. Change is ongoing.			
3. Change is mostly good.			
4. Change is something I have no control over.			
5. Change is something that happens to me.			
6. Change is something I choose to actively participate in.			
7. Change is always hard.			
8. Change must be managed to be effective.			
9. A person can never prepare enough for change.			
10. Change always presents opportunities.			

Figure 26 Perspectives on Change Quick Self-Assessment©, Change Readiness Training, Workplace Education 2017

(From Workplace Education Manitoba, Change Readiness Toolkit, Lesson Plan CR—What is Change—p. 28, 2017)

Tips on Communicating a Change Initiative

Since many people have a visceral reaction and assume the worst when they hear the word "change," we recommend encouraging everyone involved in a workplace civility initiative to replace the word *change* with the word *learning* and to focus on the positive, as well as on the end-in-mind goals and outcomes, of the initiative. Some tips on how to vocalize and present a change initiative to solicit more positive responses from your team are provided in Chapter 10, *Tools You Can Use*. For example:

- Avoid calling your initiative a change initiative, call it a "Ready to Learn," or XYZ Workplace Civility Project. Maybe it's an "Employee Engagement Program" or your "Building a Better Workplace Initiative," whatever you like; just try not to put the word change in the title.
- Instead of saying, "As a result of market changes and global trends, we all have to change. We need to work faster and be more agile," say, "We can build on our current skills and take this opportunity to learn as we adapt to trends and market shifts."

- Don't say, "You need to change how you work," say, "Learning how to work differently will make you more efficient."
- Rather than saying, "You are all required to attend change management training," say, "The continuous learning course we're all taking is going to help us manage whatever comes our way."
- Employees are more inclined to get excited about learning opportunities versus requirements to change, and people usually like knowing what the benefit of the change/learning will be. For example, say, "We can all reduce our daily stress by learning how to manage our time better. Attendance requested: Learning opportunity for supervisors, every Tuesday 9 to 11 a.m.," versus saying, "We are wasting too much time and have to do things differently. Mandatory training for supervisors. Time management training six consecutive Tuesday mornings 9 to 11 a.m."

Chapter 3

Some common and measurable symptoms of incivility have been identified over 20 years of field work by Civility Experts Inc.

Incivility Symptoms Survey

- Persistent miscommunication, such as non-responsiveness, misunderstandings, arguments, and withholding of information
- Diminished morale and/or mood, e.g., negative attitudes, lack of energy
- Poor engagement, lowered confidence, and low trust
- Measurable lack of accountability
- Decreased productivity
- Increased lateness and laziness
- Reduced quality and quantity of output
- Diminished collaborative effort
- Increased customer service complaints, due to visible decrease in product and/or service standards
- Growing gap in alignment between personal and/or corporate goals and leadership abilities
- Lack of integrity and ethics
- Inability to adapt effectively to change

- Inability to navigate cultural and communication barriers
- Increased difficulty recruiting and hiring competent personnel
- Difficulty identifying and practicing core values
- Lowered common sense
- Failure to respond to social cues and follow social conventions
- Increased disengagement as indicated by difficulty maintaining relationships, less involvement in social, civic, and community events

There are certainly workplaces more toxic than manufacturing. And there are manufacturing organizations (e.g., Toyota) that have successfully built healthier, kinder, more civil workplaces than what is traditionally seen in the sector. Statistically, however, manufacturing is still perceived as one of the "toughest" environments. Whether people recognize "tough" as uncivil depends on a range of factors, but research suggests that relative to other industries, there is a great deal of work to do in manufacturing related to improving workplace culture.

Chapter 4

The Culture Indicator Continuum

BY MASOTTI & BAYER

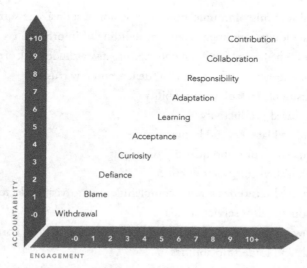

Figure 27 Incivility Symptoms Survey©, Civility Experts Inc. 2014

Chapter 5

Clearly it takes time to build communication skills and when contexts and teams are continually changing, a person must apply continuous learning in order to keep up with expectations and to be effective in various settings. Building on 20+ years' experience in manufacturing, Christian Masotti has compiled a social competence toolkit for manufacturing supervisors that includes ten communication strategies with ready-to-use checklists. Review and application of these tools can expedite a supervisor's ability to acquire critical communication skills.

Masotti Commonsense Social Competence Strategy #1: Wait for It

This strategy is about pausing—being deliberate about being present, listening, and suspending judgment.

- Pause deliberately to assess the situation.
- Resist saying anything immediately.
- Suspend your thoughts, i.e. don't make assumptions, don't jump to conclusions, set aside any bias or expectations.
- Listen to the other person.
- Pay attention to the context, e.g., what is going on around you?
- Watch the other person's nonverbal cues.
- Ask questions using a calm, polite tone.
- Avoid starting your sentences with "I" in an effort to be other-focused.
- Be self-aware. Pay attention to when you make snap judgments and work to understand why you have jumped to conclusions and then set those judgments aside.

Masotti Commonsense Social Competence Strategy #2: Just Be Nice

This strategy is about extending common courtesies and choosing to be kind.

- Pause, wait...take a breath, compose yourself, think about what you will say or do BEFORE you do it.

- Assume the best about others; try to set aside any personal issues, history with the individual, personal needs, known biases, etc.
- Consider social protocol. What do the social rules (written or unwritten) suggest is the appropriate response or behavior in this setting and/or situation?
- Think about what you want to happen next, e.g., how do you want to be perceived, how do you want the other person to feel, what do you want the outcome of the interaction/communication to be?
- Consider the time and place, e.g., is this the right time for the communication? Should you go somewhere private? Do you need a third party as witness? Does the other party need time to compose him or herself?
- Be kind.
  - Choose words and/or actions that show you at your best and do not cause harm to the other person.
  - Make eye contact as a way of acknowledging others.
  - Extend general greetings, e.g., say hello.
  - Maintain a calm and moderate tone, e.g., don't yell.
  - Avoid swearing.
- Close with a verbal or physical handshake, e.g., shake hands, say thank you for X, look the person in the eye, or acknowledge and close the interaction verbally, e.g., say, "So, we are all good then?" or "See you tomorrow then" or something to show you anticipate a positive and future interaction.

Masotti Commonsense Social Competence Strategy #3:
Get Out There and Talk to People

This strategy is about being intentional in how you engage with others socially.

- Always keep your head up when passing others or walking through a workspace, halls, parking lot, etc.
- Even if you don't know people, make it your habit to glance at them. Practice noticing things about people—what they're wearing, expressions, etc.
- Practice keeping an approachable, friendly look on your face.

- Be deliberate about exhibiting open postures: don't sit with your arms crossed, take your hands out of your pockets, remove sunglasses when talking to people indoors, extend an open palm for a handshake.
- When you know people (even if you don't know their names) make eye contact and smile.
- If you can't stop to talk, wave or nod hello, but don't ask a question such as, "How are you?" while you continue walking or moving.
- If you have time to stop and chat, stop. Turn your shoulders square with the other person, greet him or her, move to within 24 inches of the other person, and engage. Set aside all other distractions while you do so.
- If you have to break eye contact or move your attention to someone or something else for a minute, e.g., check your watch, or acknowledge another person, say, "excuse me" before you do it, or say, "sorry about that" after you do it.
- As you are chatting, make it a point to focus on the other person. Ask him or her questions and wait for the answers. Try to avoid talking about yourself.
- If you didn't shake hands when you greeted the person, and when context and culture suggest it's appropriate, extend an exit handshake.
- If you are legitimately busy, don't stop and pretend to pay attention. Simply state that you are glad to see the person, but are unable to visit at this time, and then wish the person a happy day and move on.

Masotti Commonsense Social Competence Strategy #4: Apply Continuous Learning to Connect with People

This strategy is about recognizing that every interaction is a learning opportunity.

- Treat people with respect from the beginning so that when you need to approach them for help, they see you as someone they can trust who values them.

- Assume that someone, at some time, somewhere has experienced this same situation.
- Assume that you are not the only person to have an idea.
- Always ask the people doing the job—ask them directly, face-to-face.
- Approach people at the appropriate time.
- Be respectful in your tone, don't assume people have an obligation to help you just because you are a supervisor.
- Ask targeted questions, i.e., not open-ended.
- Admit you need help.
- Listen for an answer—don't interrupt, don't criticize or apply your personal biases, opinions, or beliefs.
- Don't dismiss anyone. You never know what information will be useful down the road. Even if the information being shared at the time is not relevant, use the interaction as an opportunity to build rapport and trust.
- Consider that one person may not have all the answers, but the collective probably does.
- Acknowledge the sharing of information. Let the person sharing with you know you appreciate their help.
- Give credit when you use the information down the road.
- Share the information with others. Don't hoard it now that you have it.
- Avoid going back to the same person more than once, as this can cause strain within the team. Instead build a relationship with each member of the team. This builds credibility.

Masotti Commonsense Social Competence Strategy #5: Always Tell the Truth

This strategy is about relational wealth. If you want to build trust, here are some communication habits you should adopt:

- Make it a point to be honest with everyone—not just some people.
- Be consistent, i.e. always tell the truth—don't pick and choose when to be honest.

- Be honest when delivering both good and bad news.
- Be direct and tell the whole truth versus a piece or version of the truth, e.g., instead of saying you are being fired for lateness, an indirect version is saying, "You know, lateness is one of the metrics we watch."
- Assume the best of people, but don't immediately trust everything people say. Ask strategic questions.
- Look people in the eye when you are communicating the truth.
- Be deliberate in your communication—choose your words carefully and say exactly what you mean. Don't sugarcoat or be vague.
- Avoid pretending you have authority or power you don't have—be honest about your abilities and influence.
- Do your due diligence before making promises—ensure you can follow through before you say what you can and will do.
- Pick an appropriate time to be truthful.
- Consider privacy and confidentiality.
- Monitor your tone—don't be harsh.
- Avoid apologizing for telling the truth, e.g., "I'm sorry to have to tell you X, but…"
- Give people a minute to absorb what you are telling them.
- Keep being truthful, even when others are dishonest, and/or even when no one seems to notice. People do notice, and there is often documentation to support your efforts.

Masotti Commonsense Social Competence Strategy #6: Ask Strategic Questions

This strategy is about acknowledging that you can't know everything; you must be able to ask for help.

- See people as resources. Assume you can learn from them.
- Be clear in your own mind about what exactly you need to know—what information are you seeking?
- Watch for the appropriate time to approach someone to ask questions, e.g., don't bother employees right before lunch or during lunch or breaks. This is their personal time and they may resent

your intrusion. Consider approaching them at the end of the shift or just after a break or lunch.

- Consider privacy and confidentiality.
- Do not interrupt when the other person is talking.
- Don't assume you already know the answer to the question you are asking.
- Don't assume that the answer is correct or factual. Be sure.
- Don't assume that only one person has the answer or information you seek. Ask more than one person if possible.
- Don't assume that one person speaks for the whole group.
- Monitor your postures and nonverbal communication when listening, e.g., avoid condescending or impatient gestures.
- Listen with TING.
- Ask a specific question. Start with one question only. Avoid bombarding the person with many questions at once.
- Choose a specific question for a specific purpose. For example: Ask a "how is your day" question to gauge morale or attitude.
  - Ask a "get to the point" question to hold someone accountable for misbehavior.
  - Ask a "what would happen if" question to get someone to share information or help resolve a problem.
- Don't expect a thank you and don't say things like, "You owe me one." Extend the gesture with no expectation of reciprocity.

Masotti Social Competence Strategy #7: Build Resilience (Learn to Take a Punch)

This strategy is about being of strong will, staying positive, and not taking things too personally.

- Show people how the work they do is valued on the job, i.e. why is enduring the hardship worth it?
- Make people aware of the types of challenges they may face on the job.
- Provide opportunities for people to see how others managed those challenges in the past.

- Build your own resilience. Model resilient behavior. For example:
  ○ Have a positive attitude.
  ○ Name your fears and face them.
  ○ Set small achievable personal goals on an ongoing basis so that you can experience success.
  ○ Encourage others, i.e. foster optimism.
  ○ Don't take yourself too seriously. Have a sense of humor.
  ○ Take advantage of social support around you. Ask for help when you need it.
- Encourage autonomy.
- Provide opportunities to practice coping strategies.
- Build "time out" opportunities into daily routine, i.e., make sure people get breaks.
- Incorporate positive language, i.e. affirmations, into workplace slogans and mottos.
- Provide team support, e.g., buddy and mentor programs.

Masotti Commonsense Social Competence Strategy #8: Foster Collaboration

This strategy is about how to build engagement and rapport.

- Be approachable.
- Don't take yourself too seriously.
- Be able to say, "I don't know."
- Be transparent.
- Assume there are people in the room smarter than you are.
- Acknowledge the experience, skills, and credentials of others.
- Be curious, ask questions.
- Ask for help.
- Take notes, show that you are serious about the information you are seeking.
- Review the processes that support collaboration.
- Offer support, with no strings attached.
- Be honest about what you know.
- Share what you know.

- Stick to the facts when you can and avoid opinions.
- Thank others who share with you.
- Credit others with information they share with you that you pass on.
- Strive to exceed expectations, i.e. give more than is required.
- Implement process to ensure that all collaborators have an opportunity to share.
- Set ground rules for communication in collaborative settings.
- Invite varied opinions and discussion—disagreement is sometimes a good thing.
- Encourage wild ideas, creativity, and innovation.
- Create a psychologically safe environment where others feel free to speak.
- Maintain confidentiality where applicable.

Masotti Commonsense Social Competence Strategy #9: Be Hardy

This strategy is about recognizing your physical and mental limitations and planning for them.

- Anticipate and plan for a physically demanding environment. Consider what you and/or your team need to work well, related to:
  - Noise
  - Deadlines
  - Moving equipment
  - Moving vehicles
  - Ventilation: quality and noise associated with it
  - Repetitive motion
  - Safety equipment that hinders movement
  - Physical barriers to communication
  - Tight spaces
  - Large, open spaces
  - Difficulty related to equipment
  - Range of motion required
  - Time standing
  - Distance to areas you need to go to on the job, e.g., parking to work site

- ○ Availability of washrooms
- ○ Allowable breaks
- ○ Allergens
- ○ Chemicals
- ○ General morale
- ○ Temperature in the room
- ○ Availability of food and water
- ○ Availability of first aid or emergency equipment
- Take care of your personal needs:
  - ○ Sleep when you can and for a reasonable amount of time.
  - ○ Keep up with regular body maintenance: dentist, eye doctor, doctor.
  - ○ Have supply of any required medications on hand.
  - ○ Exercise regularly.
  - ○ Follow a healthy diet.
  - ○ Practice effective stress management.
  - ○ Practice good hygiene, e.g., hair, nails, shaving, etc.
  - ○ Make it a habit to keep clothes clean and in good repair.
  - ○ Maintain safety standards, e.g., wear safety equipment.
- Watch for typical "look and behavior" when you/or others are doing the job. If there is variance, or off-standard look and behavior, consider if that behavior is impacting performance. If it is, you need to address what you are seeing.
  - ○ You don't need to know the reason, you just identify and call out the behavior e.g., to prevent an injury, etc.
  - ○ Ask questions to discover cause of off-standard behavior, e.g., due to:
    - Drugs
    - Alcohol
    - Nervous breakdown
    - High stress
    - External situation, e.g., personal trauma
    - Illness
    - Depression
    - Hunger
    - Exhaustion
    - Distress

Masotti Commonsense Social Competence Strategy #10: Be Responsible

This strategy is about being an adult at work—recognizing you are accountable and approaching your work with maturity.

- Run your own race: Decide what you want out of life and make a plan to achieve it.
- Establish personal standards such as:
  - Morning routine
  - Daily exercise
  - Eating healthy
  - Only take jobs that pay minimum of X.
  - Do not engage in, or endorse, illegal activity.
  - Pay what I owe.
- Establish personal policies, such as:
  - Do not lie.
  - Always do more than is expected.
  - Always consider how my actions will impact others.
  - Never steal.
  - Always save someone else some hardship or misery if I can.
  - Give without expecting anything in return.
- Clarify expectations of others.
- Make promises, but only if I can keep them.
- Learn to say no.
- Learn to apologize.
- Accept compliments.
- Accept apologies from others.
- Invite feedback.
- Learn from mistakes.
- Forgive myself for mistakes.
- Accept that I can't fix/help/save everyone; people have to learn to take responsibility for themselves.
- Be sure I know what my specific responsibilities are, i.e. job tasks.
- Take ownership of my own learning.

SAMPLE JOB DESCRIPTION

Job description	ABC motor company					ALERT	
Windshield Wiper install							
Steps							

Steps		ALERT	
1	Grasp driver wiper.		
2	Grasp driver wiper arm.		
3	Slide and secure driver wiper into end of wiper arm and place assembly on table.		
4	Grasp passenger wiper.		
5	Grasp driver wiper arm.		
6	Slide and secure driver wiper into end of wiper arm.		
7	Grasp drive wiper assembly and walk to unit (vehicle).		
8	Press end of passenger wiper arm assembly on passenger wiper motor stud. Ensure wiper is on locator line on windshield.	QUALITY	
9	Place end of passenger wiper arm assembly on driver wiper motor stud. Ensure wiper is on locator line on windshield.	QUALITY	
10	Grasp two nuts from apron and hand start on wiper motor studs.	QUALITY	
11	Walk to DC gun and remove gun from holster.		
12	Return to unit and secure passenger nut and then driver nut—ensure torque is correct by green light on gun.	QUALITY	
13	Place DC gun back in holster.		
14	Remove two stud covers from apron and snap in place over passenger and driver stud/nut assembly.		

Reviewed by team member	Supervisor	Date reviewed	Super-intendant Reviewed	Document created on
		12/5/2019		6/9/2019

Revisions	
2/2/2019	Quality alert added on step 10. Nuts to be hand started to prevent cross threading.
########	Quality alert added on step 12. Ensure green light is present when done securing wiper to prevent cross threads or loose wipers.
3/5/2019	Additional clarification on steps 8 and 9. Wipers to be placed on windshield locator lines to ensure proper alignment of wipers.

Figure 28 Sample Job Description, Masotti, 2018

SAMPLE KAIZEN DOCUMENT FOR building platform for sporting event.	
Problem statement 1). Steel tables are too heavy. 2). Injuries occurring from stepping on seats. 3). Awkward reach when installing stands. 4). Requires eight team members 2 hours to complete. **Goals statement** 1). By November 30, 2019 provide plan and estimate project completion. 2). Eliminate injury incidents. 3). Reduce number of team members required to install. 4). Reduce amount of time required to install. **Type of wastes identified:** • Motion • Transport • Defects **Root Cause:** 1). Tables and materials are heavy. 2). Stands are awkward to position ergonomically. 3). Financing request has not been completed to change. **Root cause solutions:** 1). Replace tables with lighter material. 2). Provide lighter stands and operating procedures to eliminate awkward reach. 3). Provide costs estimate and timeline to be completed.	**Counter Measure #1: Manager X** to provide lighter material and design. **Counter Measures #2 and #3: Manager Y** responsible for building stands that allow install without standing on seats. Lighter tables will eliminate awkward heavy reach. **Counter Measure #4:** Create new SOP to instruct a four-member team for installation with lighter tables. **Follow-up results:** Suggestion implemented and new media tables and stands were built. New SOP created for four-member team for installation outlining risks involved in job safety analysis. Risks involved installing media tables greatly reduced and no injuries reported since plan implemented, Task takes four team members 1 hour to install compared to eight team members taking 2 hours to install. **Savings:** Before 8 team members × 2 hours at $22.15 × 80 events equaled $28,160 After 4 team members × 1 hour at $22.15 × 80 events equals $7,040 Savings of $21,120 per year Note: Zero injuries reported since new plan was implemented.

Figure 29 Sample Kaizen Document, Masotti, 2019

Chapter 5

Listening with "TING" (the ancient Chinese secret—TING): This symbol effectively illustrates what's involved when you're completely engaged in listening. Listening with TING enables us to hold a much higher quality of conversation and communication. We become engaged more intently in what the other person is telling us. This enables us to listen deeply for their meaning. When we bring our hearts, minds, ears, and eyes into the exchange, we obtain a much better result. The Chinese character for listen, "TING," captures the full spirit of listening. The upper left part of the symbol stands for ear—our ears to hear the words the speaker is saying. The lower left-hand part of the symbol represents "king" or "dominant one," indicating that hearing the words through our ear is the most important part of the listening process. In the upper right-hand part of the symbol, we see "mind." Our minds aid in understanding the words the speaker is saying and the message they contain. Below that is the eye, which allows us to see any nonverbal messages the speaker might be sending. In the bottom right-hand side is heart, and above that, the almost horizontal line translates to "one" or "to become of one." This tells us that if we listen in this way, with our ears, mind, eyes, and heart, we can become of one heart. Most of us focus on our own internal dialogue versus that with the speaker. And it's not that we don't care or we don't want to listen, but we're responding or thinking how we will respond before truly hearing the speaker generally occurs. Often, we miss the whole point that the speaker is attempting to make. So, utilizing the practice of listening with "TING" will encompass all aspects of deep quality communication if given the chance. http://wvearlychildhood.org/resources/B1Handout1.pdf

Foundational Skills for Successful Negotiating

Pre-training Assessment

Oral Communication Self-Assessment—Check the Box That Applies to You.

I can...	Yes	Somewhat	No
Ask routine questions to obtain information.			
Understand short messages and communicate the information to others.			
Give simple instructions or facts to others on a familiar topic.			
Listen to others without interrupting.			
Use appropriate body language (e.g., smiling, nodding, making eye contact) while having a conversation.			
Ask complex questions to get the appropriate information.			
Communicate with others to resolve minor conflicts, such as customer complaints.			

Figure 30 Oral Communication Self-Assessment©, Workplace Education Manitoba 2014

I can...	Yes	Somewhat	No
Communicate with others to coordinate work or resolve problems.			
Express my opinions and ideas clearly and concisely.			
Restate information that is presented orally.			
Train or give clear instructions to a coworker.			
Give a brief presentation to a small group.			
Lead routine meetings (e.g. weekly team meetings).			
Follow complex oral instructions to complete a task.			
Explain difficult subject matter using detailed examples.			
Give yourself 3 points for every Yes, 2 points for every Somewhat, and 1 point for every No.			
Total			

Figure 30 Continued

Total possible score is 45. If your score is lower than 37, it is recommended that you review the foundations for successful negotiating.

Working with Others Self-Assessment—Check the Box That Applies to You.

I can....	Yes	Somewhat	No
Organize my work tasks within a set of priorities.			
Take initiative by doing what needs to be done before being asked.			
Work cooperatively with a partner or team to complete tasks.			
Coordinate my work with the work of my colleagues to complete group projects.			
Complete my assigned work on time so that team deadlines are met.			
Complete my fair share of tasks when working with a partner or team.			
Follow directions from my partner or team members as required.			
Give directions to my partner or team members as required.			
Participate in making group decisions by contributing my ideas and suggestions.			
Contribute to making decisions cooperatively and settling differences respectfully.			

Figure 31 Working with Others Self-Assessment©, Workplace Education Manitoba 2014

I can....	Yes	Somewhat	No
Improve my work based on suggestions and advice I receive from my partner or other team members.			
Help build an open and trustworthy work environment by encouraging others to participate in activities.			
Lead by setting a good example for the people around me.			
Make decisions that I feel others can respect.			
Provide constructive feedback to help others improve their work.			
Take the lead in coordinating my colleagues' tasks in a group project.			
Encourage group interactions and maintain a positive atmosphere within my team.			
Give yourself 3 points for every Yes, 2 points for every Somewhat and 1 point for every No.			
Total			

Figure 31 Continued

Total possible score is 51. If your score is lower than 43, it is recommended that you review the foundations for successful negotiating.

Thinking Skills Self-Assessment—Check the Box That Applies to You.

I can....	Yes	Somewhat	No
Identify the cause of a problem when I have all the necessary information given to me.			
Follow existing procedures or instructions to identify solutions to a problem (e.g., the steps for fixing a broken machine).			
Find information from a variety of sources (such as equipment manuals, policies, and procedures) that will help me understand the problem and identify solutions.			
Use problem solving experiences I had in the past to help me identify solutions to current problems.			
Recognize key facts and issues related to a problem (e.g. identify answers to who, what, when, where, why, and how).			
Identify and evaluate the pros and cons of each potential solution.			

Figure 32 Thinking Skills Self-Assessment©, Workplace Education Manitoba 2014

I can....	Yes	Somewhat	No
Make adjustments to existing workplace procedures to help solve a problem (set procedures may not address every type of problem).			
Evaluate how well a solution worked.			
Make decisions when following existing procedures or policies.			
Use my knowledge and past experiences to help me make decisions.			
Consider all the relevant information available before making a decision.			
Decide which of several options is most appropriate.			
Explain why I chose a particular decision.			
Complete tasks by their level of importance that have been organized for me.			
Complete tasks by their level of importance that I have organized on my own.			
Use tools such as calendars, agendas, and to-do lists to help me organize my tasks.			
Coordinate my work with the work of my coworkers (e.g., make a schedule for using a shared piece of equipment).			
Deal with interruptions so that they do not interfere with my work schedule.			
Give yourself 3 points for every Yes, 2 points for every Somewhat, and 1 point for every No.			
Total			

Figure 32 Continued

Total possible score is 54: If your score is lower than 46, it is recommended that you review the foundations for successful negotiating.

The Honey, the Bear, the Chopper, and Brainstorming in a Team

Here is a story to illustrate G.R.O.U.P concept for when working with a group to generate new ideas, brainstorm and/or solve problems.

This is a story about the Pacific Power and Light Company in the U.S. They had a problem with ice forming on the electrical wires after snowstorms. The ice had to be removed, or over time the weight of the ice may have broken the electrical lines. The manual process was slow, tedious, and dangerous.

Pacific Power and Light therefore gathered some brainstorming teams to help solve the issue. The teams gathered consisted of people from different departments in the company. There were linesmen, managers, secretaries, and supervisors. It was said that even the mailroom personnel were invited.

During one of the breaks, one of the linesmen shared with some of the participants about how he had come face-to-face with a big, brown bear when he was servicing the power lines, and how he narrowly escaped being mauled by it.

When they returned for the meeting, someone suggested training the brown bears to climb the poles to shake off the ice from the wires. Brown bears were very common in the areas that had this issue and they were strong enough to cause the poles to shake when they climbed them. The group joked and threw out some ideas, and someone suggested putting honey pots at the top of the poles to entice the bears to climb them.

The group then started to discuss how to put the pots of honey at the top of the poles to entice bears to climb the poles. Several seemingly unworkable or outlandish ideas were discussed, and at one point, someone threw out the idea of using helicopters to do the job. As the group was thinking about the resources it would take to place pots of honey at the top of every electrical pole and whether it would work, a secretary in the meeting pointed out that the downwash from the helicopters could possibly break the ice and blow it off the wires.

There was silence, and then the team started to realize that it could work. They tested the idea and it proved to be a good one. Today, all Pacific Power and Light has to do to remove ice from the wires is to charter a helicopter to fly at low altitude above the electrical wires and the downwash from the helicopter does all the work. Linesmen no longer have to risk their lives to climb the electrical poles.

Imagine if someone had:

- started to laugh at the person who suggested training the bears to shake the poles; or
- ridiculed the idea of putting pots of honey at the top of the poles (because you will still have to climb up the poles to refill them when the bears finish the honey); or

- thought that the power lines department should be able to come out with a solution by themselves, since they should know their job better than anyone else.

Any of these or any other negative comments could have stopped more ideas from following. Fortunately, this was not what happened that day.

Moral of the Story

If you are building a team, or leading in a brainstorming session, you may want to keep the G.R.O.U.P. concept in mind.

G.R.O.U.P. Brainstorming Concept

1. **Go** for quantity.
   "The law of large numbers—the more ideas you have, the higher the chance of getting a good one."
   It does not mean that only people with relevant experience can come out with good ideas. Sometimes people who do not have too much information are able to come out with solutions that are simple, yet effective. Generally, the more ideas you have during idea generation, the better it is.
2. **Record** every single idea.
   Appoint someone to take notes as the team discusses. Record every idea that is being thrown out, regardless of who comes up with the idea. When we note down every single idea, we will not forget any one of them, especially those that seem silly at first. Another important point is building on another person's idea instead of putting the idea down at this stage.
3. **Outlaw** judgment.
   During the brainstorming session, focus on idea generation and idea selection. Leave judgment to a later time when evaluating the ideas. "Mine the gold" in other people's ideas and build on the ideas of others instead of putting them down.
4. **Unleash** crazy thoughts.

No matter how crazy an idea may seem, just throw it out and get it recorded. Remember rule number 1—the more ideas you have, the more chances of getting a good one. Some ideas may bring out other ideas. So just let it go!

5. **Period** of incubation

   If time permits, restrict the session to just generating ideas. Record all the ideas, regardless of whether they seem logical or sane. Sleep on it. Let your brain soak in all the information and allow some time to pass before the group meets again. Review which are the good ideas that can work and which are the ones to be discarded. The power of the subconscious can do wonders. Sometimes during the incubation period, when you least expect it, a good idea may just spring forth![16]

Chapter 6

Clues and Cues—A Checklist for Nonverbal Communication

Signs that you have someone's attention:

- Smiling
- Nodding
- Eyebrows raised
- Saying, "Yes, please go on…"
- Leaning forward
- He or she is actively listening
- He or she is so excited to talk to you that they interrupt or finish your sentences

Signs that someone is losing interest:

- His or her eyes are wandering, looking over your shoulder, not making eye contact, looking down or at their watch

---

[16] Anergy. n.d. "Leading Team Brainstorming: How to Lead a Team Brainstorming Session." http://singaporeteambuilding.com/teambuilding/brainstorming-in-a-team.htm.

- Fidgeting
- Pursed lips or closed-mouth smile
- He or she is whispering or doing something other than listening to you
- Yawning or stretching
- He or she interrupts you or changes the subject

Signs that someone is uncomfortable or feeling awkward:

- Pacing
- Rising or shifting away from you
- Leaving the area or room completely
- Fidgeting
- Head lowered, no eye contact
- Shoulders rounded, closed posture
- Blushing
- Profuse sweating
- Trembling
- Complaints of nausea or headache or just not looking as though they feel good
- Talking too much or not at all
- Not eating or drinking or just eating and/or drinking

Signs that someone does not believe you or is not "buying in":

- Repeating themselves, "saying," "yeah, yeah...." Or "sure, sure, okay...yeah";
- saying, "yes" with their mouth but "no" with their body language Not asking any questions at all, signaling that they've already made up their minds
- Arms crossed

Signs that someone is not being entirely honest:

- Changes in the voice's pitch, rate of speech or volume of speech
- Hesitation when speaking

- Decreased or increased eye contact
- Hands moving to cover the eyes or mouth
- Nervous movements of hands, feet, or legs; twitching of eye
- Saying things that don't make sense or suddenly changing the subject

People Treatment Self-Assessment

By L. Bayer, Civility Experts Inc. All rights reserved.

• Posture, e.g., I present myself (physically) as open-minded, ready to engage, and approachable
• Time management—I show that I understand time is a valuable resource, e.g., don't waste my time or time of others, be on time
• Expectations, e.g., have clear expectations for oneself and for others
• Treat people fairly, e.g., equal opportunity, use same criteria to measure equally, etc.
• Honesty, e.g., be honest, tell the whole truth whenever possible

• Tone, e.g., I consider tonal elements when I interact verbally with others including:
  ○ Pace
  ○ Word choice
  ○ Volume
  ○ Timing
  ○ Privacy/confidentiality
  ○ Emotionality
  ○ Impact
  ○ Relationship, e.g., accountability and familiarity
  ○ Cultural nuances
  ○ Risk, e.g., perceptions related to gender
  ○ Expectations of listener, e.g., generational aspects
  ○ Mode of communication, e.g., face-to-face, phone, etc.

• Indication of bias, e.g., Am I aware that I change my approach depending who I am interacting with?
• Common courtesy, e.g., eye contact, handshake, proximity, smile, introductions, please, thank you, offering food or beverage, etc.
• Care with word choice e.g., consider frame of reference
• Perspectives on role, rank, status, and contribution
• Communication approach, e.g., formal versus informal, conversational versus legal, personal versus professional

Figure 33 Positive People Treatment Self-Assessment©, Civility Experts Inc. 2018

- Willingness to adapt to individual need, e.g., if someone needs supports due to physical or physiological barriers
- Perception of differences, i.e., do I see differences as advantages or as barriers?
- Ability to show respect, e.g., by interacting in a way that leaves the other person feeling valued (I understand that respect is not something people need to earn; we are all deserving of respect because we are human beings)
- Ability to build rapport, i.e., ease and flow of interaction
- Response in stressful or emotional settings, e.g., Do I stay calm? Do I help others be calm? Can I exercise restraint?
- Ability to build trust and to be perceived as trustworthy
- Openness, authenticity and vulnerability
- Ability to effectively interpret verbal, nonverbal, tonal, and contextual cues
- Situational awareness, i.e., recognize factors that might impact people
- Ability to adapt social style appropriately
- Cultural competence, i.e., recognize, adapt, and work with differences
- Emotional intelligence, i.e., be aware of my own issues and hot buttons
- Ability to empathize and share perspective
- Ego, i.e., attitude about one's own importance
- Humility, i.e., ability to acknowledge gifts and contributions of others over focusing on one's own gifts, talents, and contributions
- Willingness to learn
- Patience to listen
- Willingness to apologize
- Curiosity, i.e., interest in learning and asking questions
- Readiness to forgive, i.e., accept apologies with grace
- Recognition of human condition, i.e., acknowledge that I can't always understand or know what another person is experiencing
- Generosity, i.e., ability to give with no expectation of return
- Systems thinking, i.e., ability to consider impact of actions and decisions
- Social acuity, i.e., ability to assess and interpret interpersonal connections and cost, benefits, and consequences of same
- Values, e.g., can I articulate my values if necessary, and do I live my values?
- Ability to acknowledge and celebrate achievements and contributions of others
- Positive attitude, i.e. look for the best in people and in situations
- Responsibility, i.e. take care of myself, don't blame others or expect other to manage me (my daily life or actions or activities)
- Accountability, i.e., own my own tasks and decisions
- Service-orientation, i.e., do I show through my actions that I am "other-focused" and can put needs of others before my own needs and wants when appropriate or required?

Figure 33 Continued

Chapter 7

The Culture Indicator Continuum

BY MASOTTI & BAYER

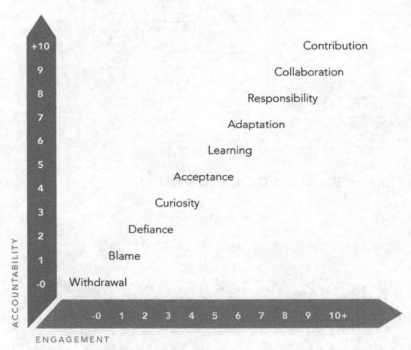

Figure 34 The Culture Indicator Continuum by Masotti and Bayer

Tools You Can Use

Blooms Verb Chart[17]—The following is a list of measurable action verbs that can be used when you need to be specific, e.g., when giving directions.

---

[17]J. Shabatura. September 18, 2014. "Blooms Taxonomy Verb Chart," *Teaching Innovation and Pedagogical Support.* https://tips.uark.edu/blooms-taxonomy-verb-chart/.

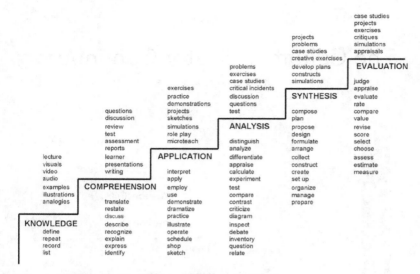

Figure 35 Blooms Verb Chart, Sabatura, 2014

Chapter 8

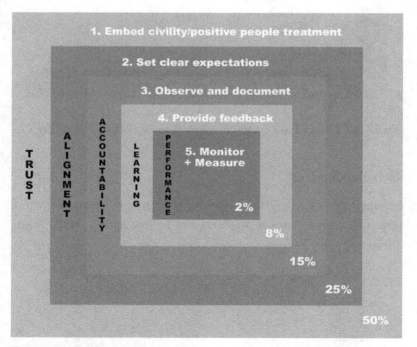

*Figure 36 Civility as Continuous Improvement Model © Masotti &
Bayer 2020*

About the Authors

Christian Masotti

With 20 years of hands-on manufacturing experience, Christian Masotti has witnessed time and time again how incivility can impact business. Having worked with—among others—the big three auto manufacturers including Ford, Chrysler, and Toyota, Christian understands how failure to address the people side of change appropriately, that is, teach "people treatment," results in manufacturing workplaces continuing to experience high turnover, poor morale, and lowered profitability. As a professional athlete who now supervises event conversions for Maple Leaf Sports & Entertainment, Masotti has also experienced how incivility can impact professional sports, sports-related organizations, human resources, volunteers, and frontline workers. To create tools and training to support positive people-focused change in workplaces, Masotti teamed up with internationally acclaimed workplace Civility Experts Inc. CEO Lewena Bayer. Together, the duo has devised a range of civil communication and interpersonal strategies customized for application in manufacturing organizations via books, online courses, live training, and keynote presentations.

Lewena Bayer

For more than 20 years, Lewena Bayer has been internationally recognized as the leading expert on civility at work. With a focus on social intelligence and culturally competent communication, the team at Civility Experts, which includes 501 affiliates in 48 countries, has supported 100s of organizations in building better workplaces. In addition to her role as CEO of international civility training group, Civility Experts Inc., Lew is a 16-time published author, chair of the International Civility Trainers' Consortium, president of The Center for Organizational Cultural Competence, and founder of the In Good Company Etiquette Academy Franchise Group as well as the HighStyle Image Company. Lew is an international advocate for Aegis Trust, a UK-based organization focused on peace education, and is education chair for Global Goodwill Ambassadors. Recently, Dr. Bayer (Hon.) has been named Ambassador for the Global Knowledge Exchange and as Lead Master Educator in Global Teachers Academy.

Index

OTHER TITLES IN THE HUMAN RESOURCE MANAGEMENT AND ORGANIZATIONAL BEHAVIOR COLLECTION

- *Strengths Oriented Leadership: The World Through Bee Glasses* by Matt L. Beadle
- *Transforming the Next Generation Leaders: Developing Future Leaders for a Disruptive, Digital-Driven Era of the Fourth Industrial Revolution (Industry 4.0)* by Sattar Bawany
- *Level-Up Leadership: Engaging Leaders for Success* by Michael J. Provitera
- *The Truth About Collaborating: Why People Fail and How to Succeed* by Dr. Gail Levitt
- *Uses and Risks of Business Chatbots: Guidelines for Purchasers in the Public and Private Sectors* by Tania Peitzker
- *Three Key Success Factors for Transforming Your Business: Mindset, Infrastructure, Capability* by Michael Hagemann
- *Hiring for Fit: A Key Leadership Skill* by Janet Webb
- *Successful Recruitment: How to Recruit the Right People For Your Business* by Stephen Amos
- *Uniquely Great Essentials for Winning Employers* by Lucy English
- *The Relevance of Humanities to the 21st Century Workplace* by Michael Edmondson
- *Untenable: A Leader's Guide to Addressing the Big Issues That Are Ignored, Falsely Explained, or Inappropriately Tolerated* by Gary Covert
- *Chief Kickboxing Officer Applying the Fight Mentality to Business Success* by Alfonso Asensio
- *Transforming the Next Generation Leaders: Developing Future Leaders for a Disruptive, Digital-Driven Era of the Fourth Industrial Revolution (Industry 4.0)* by Sattar Bawany

Concise and Applied Business Books

The Collection listed above is one of 30 business subject collections that Business Expert Press has grown to make BEP a premiere publisher of print and digital books. Our concise and applied books are for...

- Professionals and Practitioners
- Faculty who adopt our books for courses
- Librarians who know that BEP's Digital Libraries are a unique way to offer students ebooks to download, not restricted with any digital rights management
- Executive Training Course Leaders
- Business Seminar Organizers

Business Expert Press books are for anyone who needs to dig deeper on business ideas, goals, and solutions to everyday problems. Whether one print book, one ebook, or buying a digital library of 110 ebooks, we remain the affordable and smart way to be business smart. For more information, please visit **www.businessexpertpress.com**, or contact **sales@businessexpertpress.com**.

CPSIA information can be obtained
at www.ICGtesting.com
Printed in the USA
BVHW090236090922
646611BV00006B/88